The Scientific M
Social Scie

Implications for Research and Application

Cho-Yee To

with a foreword by
Nathan Caplan
University of Michigan

Trentham Books
Stoke on Trent, UK and Sterling, USA

Trentham Books Limited

Westview House	22883 Quicksilver Drive
734 London Road	Sterling
Oakhill	VA 20166-2012
Stoke on Trent	USA
Staffordshire	
England ST4 5NP	

First published 2000

British Library Cataloguing-in-Publication Data
A catalogue record for this book is available from the British Library

1 85856 232 5 (paperback)

Designed and typeset by Trentham Print Design Ltd., Chester and printed in Great Britain by Cromwell Press Ltd., Wiltshire.

The Scientific Merit of the
Social Sciences
Implications for Research and Application

CONTENTS

The considerable gap between the natural sciences and the social sciences appears to have grown in recent years; the former have made strides in theory and practice while the latter continue to present a spectacle of disarray and dubious performance. I am in complete agreement with the central thesis of this study.
L.B. Curzon, Barrister at Law, Oxford

It is one thing to feel uncomfortable about the way social science research has been conducted and quite another to be able to pinpoint the source of the problem and to offer remedies and solutions. Such response can come only from someone who is an experienced student in social research and philosophy and who possesses the knowledge as well as the insights and critical acumen required to attack the problem under consideration – qualities which are eminently apparent in the works of Professor To, the author of this book.
Lik Kuen Tong, Professor of Philosophy, Fairfield University

What I find the most praiseworthy about this volume is Professor To's unapologetic and uncompromising conviction that the end of scholarly effort should not be elegant theory, but informed practice for a better world. Especially because the postmodern turn in the human and social sciences has contributed to a general malaise regarding the social relevance of research, Professor To's insistence that scholars respond constructively to social problems is most welcome. The development of a rigorous social science for such task within the academy will not be easy, since the university must be both critical of society as well as responsive to it. Nevertheless, Professor To's vision provides a compelling springboard for discussing how we might negotiate that precarious balance, and move our work, in his words, from superficiality to profundity, from triviality to comprehensiveness, from dispersive to cumulative.
Heidi Ross, Chair, Department of Education, Colgate University

Foreword

Impatience and disillusionment with the progress of research and knowledge in the social sciences as it relates to the practical problems of society is not unusual. Many people find little usable information in the literature and have come to believe that the social sciences do not serve goals outside these sciences. The judgement may sound harsh but it is accurate.

The topic is not new. Since the 1960s it has received considerable attention especially so in the earlier period. Many talk pieces were published on the topic, some research was done; and a number of blue-ribbon committees were established and international conferences were held on the application of social science results to social problems and the promotion of human betterment. Also at issue was the efficient use of government funds invested in the production of information suitable for use by planners and practitioners.

Even so, little of substance was produced. Nothing really crystallized. No generally accepted theory emerged about knowledge production in relation to the needs of social practitioners. Today the need for usable knowledge upon which to premise social programs is as great as ever, if not greater, especially in the field of education, which is main focus of Professor To's book.

Typically, the published work on the social utility of social science research has focused on issues pertaining to relevance, communicability, reliability of research findings, the channels for communication to practitioners, and such like. Some progress has been made in defining the issues beyond these more obvious concerns, such as the instrumental application of conceptual knowledge, the deliberate misuse of applicable knowledge by policy planners, and the determination of whether the problem is a poverty of usable information or one of improving its implementation.

Less obvious, but of no less importance, is the fact that many knowledge producers, particularly in the more prestigious universities, believe it a menace to their careers were they to focus on socially applicable information, and therefore ignore the pressure on the social sciences to do so. Ironically, they gain far greater professional standing by interpreting social reality as a special case of the theoretical.

Professor To steps back from these troubled and unresolved issues, and by doing so, regains a much needed perspective on the problems of the use of social science knowledge. How one defines a problem determines what is done about it. What he does is to examine some very fundamental issues to gain an accurate definition of the problem, specifically challenging the ability of social sciences to make valid predictions.

He is uniquely qualified for the task, bringing a deep understanding of the philosophy and history of science, the philosophy of education and a fingertip sensitivity to knowledge utilisation issues as they pertain to contemporary problems in education at all levels, elementary, secondary as well as higher education. The book is beautifully written and evocative.

Professor To's dissuasion of issues is particularly appropriate as a fin-de-siècle statement of what is needed to foster the social utility of the social sciences in the future.

Nathan Caplan, Professor Emeritus of Psychology and Senior Research Scientist, The University of Michigan January 2000

Preface

It has taken me seven years of teaching and testing to produce this book version of the original manuscript, involving major and minor reviews by my colleagues, students and myself of the position presented. I hope that the publication will bring the study of the validity of the social sciences to a wider readership who will examine it and generate new ideas relevant to the advancement of the social sciences and their application.

To be sure it has taken a much longer period of time to investigate the scientific nature and function of social science theories. For many years I have been working in education dealing with problems related to the upbringing of the younger generation and the expectations of the older. Growth, fulfilment, equity, equality, cost-effectiveness, value-addedness, are but a few of the challenges educators have to face. Some of these problems are perennial, and many of them are unique, but all are beyond the reach of common sense when it comes to offering a solution.

Confronted by their assignments, educators have been looking for help from modern social sciences ever since they were founded as an academic discipline in the nineteenth century. Various psychological, sociological, historical and anthropological theories and methods have been applied to the field of education for interpretation and solution of problems arising in policy, planning, administration, teaching, learning, counselling and the like.

Even so, lengthy and systematic observations confirm that the application of the social sciences to education, either uniformly or eclectically, leads to limited and inconclusive results only. The inability of the social sciences to predict and resolve educational problems in particular, which is the concern of this work, has stimulated my study of the scientific merits of the social sciences and implications for further research. Here I would mention the question to what extent social science theories depend on culture, a topic which could be dealt with only briefly in the third part of the present study, but which received more attention in an earlier book of mine.*

This study represents not so much a criticism but an attempt to find a way to make the social sciences more scientific through a series of recommendations on searching for causal relation in social research. This book can be used independently as a reference on research methodology and a review guide for the analysis of social science theories.

For the completion of the study, I wish to acknowledge the contributions made by my many students in the University of Michigan, who followed my lectures and developed highly meaningful discussions in classes and seminars. I particularly appreciate the insightful comments of three doctoral candidates who creatively used the guidelines provided to pursue case analyses, which were cited for substantiation of the arguments presented: Trevor Leutscher, who studied Skinner, Mary Jo May, who studied Piaget, and Helen Marks, who studied Kohlberg, proceeding to produce scholarly articles in their respective areas.

---

*   Cho-Yee To, *Cross-cultural Transplants; Western Social Science Theories in Chinese Societies*, Hong Kong: The Chinese University of Hong Kong 1993; Taipei: Yuan Liu Press, 1994. (Chinese and English) 439pp.

Throughout my work, I have received invaluable advice and support from several distinguished colleagues: Dr. Nathan Caplan, Professor of Psychology at the University of Michigan, who commented enthusiastically on the first draft and wrote the Foreword for this book; the late Lord Todd, Professor of Chemistry and Master of Christ's College, Cambridge, and Councillor of the Chinese University of Hong Kong, who also read the first draft and expressed his broad agreement with the study; Dr. Lik Kuen Tong, Professor of Philosophy at Fairfield University, Dr. Brian Rowan, Professor of Education at the University of Michigan and Heidi Ross, Associate Professor of Education at Colgate University, who meticulously reviewed the philosophical and educational arguments; Dr. Edward Y. Yao, Professor of Physics at the University of Michigan, Dr. Charles K. Kao, Vice-Chancellor Emeritus and Honourary Professor of Engineering at the Chinese University of Hong Kong, and my brother Cho-Fong To, Senior Consulting Engineer at the Bank of America Computing Centre, who provided invaluable help in interpreting the characteristics of the natural sciences and technology.

I am particularly indebted to Professor Witold Tulasiewicz, Fellow of Wolfson College, Cambridge for helping prepare the final draft and making several very useful suggestions which could be incorporated; Drs. Rudolf Schmerl of Michigan and L.B. Curzon of Oxford, who provided me with deeply perceptive intellectual ideas for consideration. They are colleagues of many years standing. I am also grateful to Professor John Eggleston of Trentham Books, for undertaking to publish this book.

Cho-Yee To, Ann Arbor, Michigan
January 2000

CHAPTER 1

INTRODUCTION

To date, the social sciences have had only limited success in the definition and solution of pressing social problems which without effective intervention are unlikely to abate. If knowledge generated through social science research is to be able to rectify some of the problems, the quality of this research must be substantially improved. This study of the potential of the social sciences to solve problems is motivated by a critical, yet open-minded, concern for their advancement

The considerable gap between the natural sciences and the so-called social sciences appears to have grown in recent years; the former have made considerable strides in theory and practice while the latter continue to present a spectacle of considerable disarray. Central to the causes of this state of affairs are the following:

1. An intensification of the ability of the natural sciences to utilise the advances in technology and modes of quantification.

2. A retreat of the social sciences into dogma, a failure to harness the achievements of the natural sciences in areas of methodology and a persistent refusal of social scientists to 'look inwardly' and examine their concepts of what constitutes scientific thought.

3. The reluctance of the social sciences to answer the two key questions: When does a set of hypotheses, if true, provide an explanation of why something happened? When does a collection of data confirm a given hypothesis? The answers to these questions characterise the natural sciences.

4. Semantic confusion, ambiguity of terms and a vocabulary more suitable to superstition continue to surface in a significant portion of the work of some social sciences.

The following three chapters discuss the major obstacles to sound and effective research in the social sciences and compare the modes of inquiry in the natural sciences and the social sciences, using scientific inquiry as the standard, and identify the scientific nature, or lack of it, of the latter. The fourth chapter suggests steps for redirecting the social sciences toward their promise of achieving scientific merit through the accurate observation of the cause-effect relationship of human events which can be tested. From the array of areas which lend themselves to examination, the area of learning theory is being given more especial consideration.

CHAPTER 2

THE PROBLEM

If historian Paul Kennedy's projections concerning the twenty-first century should prove correct, social scientists can anticipate numerous social problems that they can study and help solve. These problems, ranging from population growth, environmental protection and the impact of technology to racial tension, and human morality, and affecting international relations, are likely to be much more complicated and have more serious implications than those faced by yesterday's and today's social scientists and will prove more difficult to resolve.'[1]

Politicians, military leaders, social advocates, and various interest groups will always be involved in one way or another in reacting to these problems, ostensibly on behalf of the public. The legitimate aim of policy makers should ultimately be to solve problems or, at least, to prevent problems from worsening. However, supporting preventive measures based on one group's speculation about the future would not be justifiable since it could not be claimed with certainty that the problems anticipated by that group will actually arise. Would social scientists, mostly confined to academia, be willing to assume greater responsibility for finding effective ways of solving these problems once they do arise? If the response is affirmative, which would be the only honourable answer and consistent with the reasoning behind the birth of modern social sciences,[2] then the next question will be: do modern social sciences, after having accumulated over a hundred years of experience, now possess the ability to identify various social problems, understand causality in social environments, predict social change, and thus provide intelligent direction for solution?

In this regard the social sciences have so far displayed a dismal, indeed dubious record. While research and training in all branches of the social sciences continue to expand, resulting in voluminous findings and interpretations, pressing problems continue to exist, change and multiply, as if the proposals and recommendations made by economists, sociologists, psychologists, political scientists, educationists, and other social scientists have had no positive effect. The contributions of the social sciences to our understanding of our society have been inevitably ephemeral, because the nature of the social environment makes it virtually impossible to consider every permutation of events that could conceivably occur. Even if social scientists select the permutation that they anticipate will have a successful outcome, those affected by it can change their behaviour in response to the selection, which may make the alternative solution chosen no longer appropriate. The forecast itself becomes a factor in the permutation.

Often, after an economic forecast has been made, the trend takes another course; after a political projection has been announced, people change their voting behaviour, making the projection invalid. The advice of social scientists is solicited on the assumption that their judgements will be superior to the common sense of ordinary men and women. Experience has not consistently proven this assumption to be correct. In the much publicised

4

Waco, Texas, cult case, the American Attorney General acknowledged seeking advice from many experts[3] before she made her 'best informed' decision to send an army tank to fire tear gas into the Branch Davidians' compound. The ending of the 51-day drama in Texas was tragic in the extreme. Developments such as these prompt questions about the reliability and soundness of the suggestions given to the Attorney General by the unnamed psychological, behavioural, theological, and communication specialists and expert social scientists.

Another case that casts serious doubts on the reliability of social science theories is the Baby Jessica case, which has attracted national attention in the United States. In that case, Jessica's natural parents in Iowa sued to regain custody of the two-year-old, who had been raised by her adoptive parents in Michigan since she was only a few weeks old. Each side brought in psychologists, social workers, and lawyers to testify on the child's and parents' behalf. The theoretical arguments presented by both sides were meticulous, using sources prepared by scholars in support. The respective conclusions reached turned out, as would be expected, completely different. The legal arguments resulted in Jessica being returned to her biological parents. Ten months after losing custody of Jessica her adoptive parents adopted another child.[4]

Although the social sciences, which have created a vast division of studies in higher education, have been generating theories and information of various quality about societies, it is difficult to distinguish with absolute certainty the sound from the unsound, and the useful from the useless. The many fields of social studies, coming under the general umbrella of the 'social sciences', have only reluctantly been recognised as being scientific

5

– being labelled the 'soft sciences' – since they have been unable to 'produce a significant body of sure, tested knowledge'.[5] Indeed the research conducted in the more applied and problem-solving branches of the social sciences, such as education and social care, has been considered mediocre.[6]

The inability of the social sciences to generate sound knowledge and thus produce the means to predict social changes and to solve social problems has long been remarked upon.[7] In this predicative context the social sciences have been likened to the natural sciences, from which the social sciences have drawn insights, borrowed methods, and adopted terms and concepts. One major point of contrast is that the social sciences have not been able to be sufficiently scientific in conducting their inquiries. Due to the unwillingness, or inability of social scientists to commit themselves to an objectively described world view, the social sciences, unlike the natural sciences, do not possess a firm basis for communication and criticism, and for arriving at criteria for the establishment of a consensus.[8] The social sciences do seem to exhibit one or another of the characteristics of science, such as the emphasis on factual data, the employment of experimental procedures, and the use of scientific terms; at the fundamental and specific levels, however, they fall short of meeting a vital mark of true science, viz. falsifiability.[9] In other words, the social sciences have yet to attain full scientific status.[10]

The lack of substantial progress in the social sciences toward becoming truly scientific comes as a great disappointment. This is because when a new social inquiry is initially developed, it is accompanied by vigorous debate, excitement, and promise. A review of the modern history

6

of the social sciences will show that the establishment of the social sciences was inseparable from the ideas of great original thinkers, who took up the challenges of the science, pursued creative inquiries into human pheno-mena and social problems, formed new thoughts, and constructed new theories. Imposing figures such as Sigmund Freud, John Maynard Keynes, Thomas Malthus, Karl Marx, Max Weber, and more recently, Milton Friedman, B.F. Skinner and H.J. Eysenck, all have made important contributions to their respective fields.[11] Their influence has been so dominating that these social theoreticians, intentionally or unintentionally, began and continued to attract generations of students to their schools of thought, and that their names have formed the roots of many of the 'isms' in the social sciences. The general pattern of development of social science inquiry, however, shows that this usually stopped with the found-ing theorists themselves.

7

The people immediately attracted to a particular social science theorist tended to become his disciples or fol-lowers who subscribed to the fundamental ideas and pre-mises of the founding theory, and upon these premises, they conducted their own research and interpreted data. Their studies supported, expanded, or extended the founding theory. Those who disagreed with the theory would oppose it and argue against it, using ideas and theories originating with other schools or traditions. The absence of systematic attempts to test and verify the first theory in an objective and open way by either the insiders or outsiders makes it impossible to revise that theory, re-fine it, develop it, refute it, prove it false, or abandon it. Within certain camps of social science theories, there may emerge from time to time efforts to update the founding theories to make them more relevant to the constantly changing social and human condition, without, however, challenging the very foundation of each theory. Thus certain 'neo-isms' are formed. As a result, more and more theories with sub-theories on the same or similar topic have been created and co-exist, forming the multiple theory phenomenon so characteristic of the social sciences. Various contradicting social science theories contend with one another in the same field; none of these theories can claim to be closer to the truth than the others, nor can any one of them produce irrefutable proof using scientific means that the others are wrong,[12] a feature well known in conducting intelligence testing.

The advancement of social science theories usually ceases with the first generation – that of the founding theorist – or the second generation, that of the follower or revisionist, or the neo-theorist, if any, as in the cases of Neo-Marxism and Neo-Freudianism. There are three explanations for this early abandonment.

8

First, even if the theory's founder was willing to acquire more data to develop a more convincing theory, the constantly changing human and social condition would make it difficult, if not impossible, to conduct a comprehensive and systematic inquiry within his limited lifetime. Hence, the originator drew a conclusion and built a theory with only limited substantiation, the original effort of inquiry ending prematurely. It has been said that no body of knowledge comes to maturity until it is willing to challenge the authority of the founder. In the social sciences the founder's theory, although creative, usually has a previous philosophical or ideological foundation, with analyses of data derived from the pre-existing theory. Rather than proceeding forward toward the testing and formulation of this theory the data are made to fit it. In the natural sciences, by contrast, analyses of data form the foundation for the development of a theory, with natural scientists attempting to draw theory from the data obtained. Philosophy comes later.

Second, while the validity of the theory may be limited to the special temporal and social setting wherein the theory was originally formed, the rhetoric used to announce it tends to suggest that it is applicable in a larger context. In fact, to claim some form of applicability to other situations, similar or dissimilar, is the only way for a social science theory to make itself available for adoption. The utilisation of a theory to address problems arising at different points of time and in different social contexts assumes that the theory is capable of more general applicability. The assumption of extended applicability, or universality, usually held by followers and users who romanticise the function and power of the theory, virtually forecloses the possibility for the advancement of the original inquiry made.

Third, the creative mind and the profound insight of the founder and the appealing prospect of the theory impress and overwhelm many who study the original idea. The lesser intellect will be completely satisfied with becoming a footnote to the grand teaching. It is probably 'safer' to adhere than to depart, to follow than to lead, to copy than to invent. Since the definitive conclusion is thought to have been reached, what is left is interpretation and further promotion. In this way 'isms' are established and schools of thought are formed.

The results of a series of studies of several leading psychological theories reveal that the foregoing has in

9

fact been the trend. The theories concerned are those of Jean Piaget, Burrhus F. Skinner, and Lawrence Kohlberg.[13] These influential psychological and social theorists were willing to meet the challenges of a scientific movement in modern times and to pursue their research by empirical means. The sources of their empirical data, however, were clearly limited.

Piaget is perhaps best known for his stage theory of human intellectual development which is to do with the elaboration of the philosophical position of genetic epistemology, linking biological adaptation to epistemological questions about the knower and the known. The primary interest that stimulated the development of the stage theory concerned the question of how the intellect developed its complexity after the individual's birth. Piaget wanted to understand the relationship between the knower and the known. As he attempted to understand the childhood origins of human knowledge, he studied knowledge acquisition in almost every domain (e.g. logic, space, time, chance, morality, play, language, and mathematics) and a wide range of related psychological processes (e.g. reasoning, perception, imagery, memory, imitation, and action). However, there is considerable disagreement among scholars (such as D. Cohen, H.G. Furth and R. Vuyk) regarding Piaget's most important theoretical contribution.[14]

Piaget made a number of claims about the universal nature of the structure and sequence of the stages of development. Although his theory was founded upon data derived from studying European children, Piaget asserted that children of any cultural background would develop intellectually according to these stages. He believed that all societies have 'certain unique characteristics and all individuals have universal characteristics in their cognitive development. All have... a common kernel... the speed might differ, but the stages would be in the same sequence....'[15] However, Piaget never attempted to test his theory in different cultural settings. Others did attempt to provide a test of cross-cultural conservation but with the caveat that the tests were always Western in nature.[16] Indeed, his critics insist that Piaget should not have had such confidence in his findings because they are based on a relatively small number of cases and do not consider such external factors as economic and social well-being which influence children's development.

Skinner's main contribution to behaviourism was the development of the concept of the operant, a variety of behaviour which has no apparent eliciting stimulus. This led Skinner to formulate a new variety of behaviourism called operant behaviourism regarded as the systematic foundation of a field of psychology known as the experimental analysis of behaviour. This field is concerned with attempts to describe much human and animal behaviour as observable phenomena with the objective of predicting and controlling behaviour. Skinner himself had even stated that his most important contribution was 'the original experimental analysis of operant behaviour and its subsequent extension to more and more complex case'.[17]

The experiments of behaviourists usually made use of 'lower animals', mainly rats and pigeons, as subjects, but claimed that the conceptual results were fundamentally true for all organisms, including human beings. This, as one would expect, is a point of great controversy. Skinner went even further, insisting that the experimental analysis of behaviour was not the science of behaviour; 'it is the

11

philosophy of that science', and that other fields of psychology represented obstacles to establishing that goal.[18] Furthermore, Skinner implicitly claimed that behavioural techniques were universally applicable as tools for cultural engineering, giving visions of culturally engineered societies in his books *Walden Two* and *Beyond Freedom and Dignity.*

Skinner's critics as well as some supporters have suggested that Skinner was an iconoclastic promoter of the experimental analysis of behaviour.[19] Indeed, Skinner was an advocate of using behavioural methods to understand behaviour and subsequently resolve social problems manifested in behaviour.

Kohlberg's interests concerned moral reasoning, moral action, moral autonomy, moral development, and moral education. His main theoretical contribution was the postulation of six stages of moral development divided into three moral 'levels'.[20] He interviewed 84 boys from a well-off social class every three years over a period of 20 years about a series of dilemmas they were to resolve. He believed that the data he collected provided the validating evidence for the conception of his stages of development,[21] basing his claim on 'basic assumptions of cognitive-developmental approaches (leading) to the proposition that both stages and sequence in the development of moral reasoning are universal, or culturally invariant'.[22] Kohlberg confidently claimed universality for his theory. His critics, however, have objected to the exclusive use of socially upper-class Caucasian boys as the subjects during the development of the theory. Several studies have tested Kohlberg's theory in different cultural settings and also with girls for the attainment of distinctive moral 'levels'. The results have led to different interpretations.[23]

Psychology is replete with examples of 'extrapolating beyond the data' as a result of wide generalisations. At least one psychometrist, whose data on intelligence resulted from the testing of groups of officer cadets, produced generalised theories covering humans as a whole. The history of the work of Jensen, and latterly, Herrnstein and Murray, which has given aid and comfort to racists, provides examples of so-called 'universal conclusions' drawn from culture-specific tests.[24]

The building, extension, and eventual fading form a complete life cycle of a social theory. The most influential days of Piagetianism, Skinnerism, and Kohlbergism have now passed. With the political collapse of Communism, some believe that the long-lasting impact of Marxism, too, is approaching its end; but its influence on historians, such as Christopher Hill, Rodney Hilton, and philosophers, such as G. Cohen, remains strong, suggesting that the class interpretation of political development will be around for some time to come. As against that, although in the post-modern era the age of the old isms' may be over, new theories are emerging to replace them, particularly in economics. There are always some temporarily dominating social theories available for selection and adoption. These theories, old and new, operate in their time largely independently. While they draw insights and ideas eclectically from one another, there is little real communication, and usually no collaboration among their authors. Different social theories have addressed the same problems, but they use different academic languages. They may use the same academic terms, but with different definitions. Despite their appearance of being general, the nature of the social sciences is highly individualistic, the 'splendid isolation' of many economists is

13

an example in point. Thus, the lack of a long-lived research tradition and of an established mechanism for social science inquiry to amass a sound knowledge base with cumulative effect for the construction of stronger theories which will withstand the test of time is perhaps the most serious limitation of the social sciences.In economics during the 1930s through the 1960s, the Keynesian position developed around the idea that an economic system operates under uncertainty and necessarily circulates around a moving equilibrium. The central message is that maintenance of a stable economy requires governmental policy to continuously stabilise both fiscal and monetary activities. At the same time the University of Chicago school, following a European tradition, developed a free-market vision without governmental interference and monitoring.[25] Economic policies deriving from these two theoretical positions are still being implemented although no irrefutable long-term proof exists of their validity.

In the 1980s and 1990s there has been an increase in the search of 'theories' particularly those relating to classroom practice and the preparation of teachers, a popular division of recent social science research. The accessibility by non-professional parties with various degrees of expert commitment makes this an easy area for conducting small scale experiments, setting up theories and indeed introducing new practices after rapid and untested observations and trials, such as in relating pupils' school performance to teaching methods and teaching arrangements. Significant is the 'reflective practitioner' of the American educationist, David Schön, whose thesis assumes a close link between practice and 'education theory in the practice'.[26]

14

A popular procedure in social research has been to deliberate on a so-called theoretical framework, both to justify the pursuit of a topic and, supposedly, to guide the development of the research. This procedure has been made a formal requirement by several funding agencies for investigators seeking awards, as well as part of the formal training of graduate students headed for research careers. As a result, social scientists in need of such external support have to go through an extensive process of literature review looking for theories that seem relevant, interesting, and helpful to their chosen topics.

The aspiration to having a theoretical framework may erect additional barriers to advancement in the social sciences. Not that such a framework is not necessary; theory is, after all, the goal of abstraction. But theory is too often confused with speculation, definitions are too often arbitrary, subjectivity is too frequently extolled as superior to the 'delusion' of scientific objectivity, and, with only the self-announced identity (race, class, and gender) of the investigator as a reference point, the student is left as deluged with theories and their variations as with fashions in popular music and entertainment, speech, and dress. That, in fact, may be the point: the formulation of theory, even about popular culture, is too often indistinguishable from participating in it.

These concerns were illustrated by the findings of a study conducted by the author with the help of a number of colleagues. The study analyses the research designs of 79 recent doctoral research proposals in the social sciences competing for dissertation grants at a leading American research university[27] with the following results:

15

A. **33** projects made use of theory; of these

    1. **16** projects used a single theory.

        i. **8** researchers chose their topic and theory independently.

        ii. **8** researchers obtained their topic and theory from a mentor or prominent figure in the field.

    2. **17** projects used multiple theories; of these

        i. **9** researchers chose their topic and theory independently.

        ii. **8** researchers obtained their topic and theory from a mentor or prominent figure in the field.

B. **46** projects made no use of theory; of these

    1. **34** researchers chose their topic independently.

    2. **12** researchers obtained their topic from a mentor or prominent figure in the field.

Of the above total:

C. **12** researchers deliberated on the selection of the theory; of these

    1. **5** researchers intended to test the theory in the course of the research.

    2. **7** researchers did not state that their chosen theory would be empirically tested in the course of the research.

D. **67** researchers did not discuss how they selected a particular theory; of these

1. **14** researchers intended to test the theory in the course of the research.

2. **53** researchers did not intend to test the theory in the course of the research.

From the above analysis it is possible to make the following observations:

First, of the 79 doctoral research projects analysed, fewer than half adopted a theory or theories for guidance. This finding itself communicates a startling commentary on research practice and design in the social sciences. Further, of those projects that did adopt a theory, few researchers actually deliberated on why they had selected a particular theory or theories for use in their study. In other words, the researchers provided no justification why the theory was appropriate or applicable in the specific context of their project, nor did they explain the importance of the theory for the research to be conducted. This situation may signify that researchers select theories either in a way that is expedient or on an ad hoc ideological basis. In fact, of the projects that did make use of theory, almost half either obtained their topics or adopted their theoretical positions from a mentor or a prominent leader in their specialisation without justifying their suitability for the specific topic attempted. The products of such research must surely be questioned.

Second, only 12 of the research projects deliberated on the selection of the theory or theories used. If this finding is surprising, then it may well be a shock to find that only 19 of the research projects mentioned any measures that would be taken to evaluate or test the theories before use, even though theory testing is the stated objective of some of the research proposals; tested, to be sure, within a

17

specific topic. This observation suggests either that the researchers view the theories as complete and, hence, in no need of review, or that testing the adopted theory is beyond the researchers' capacity or responsibility. A direct test of a theory during the course of research may not be necessary (the application itself serves as a limited test), but only when previous empirical research has provided sufficient evidence to give the theory a high degree of correspondence between the evidence and the formulation of the theory. If the research proposals offer an accurate description of what these projects would later do, then the research projects themselves might generate 79 sets of data and conclusions, but would still be unable to make a significant contribution to the advancement of the social sciences, since they missed the opportunity to scrutinise, modify and refine, correct, or reject the knowledge and theories through using them in a different time, a different place, and a different social and cultural context.

Third, an eclectic approach and employment of multiple theories are evident in 17 of the 33 studies that use theory. When utilising a variety of theories, it is necessary to consider whether the theories complement one another, or at least do not contradict and exclude one another. The research proposals rarely address this problem explicitly.[28] On the contrary, as testimonials for adopting the theories the researchers cited many reference sources without sufficient explanation or justification, a practice which indicates laxity in social research. This finding can also be interpreted as a sign of the subjectivity in the social sciences already mentioned. The choice of theories, methods, and approaches for research may have more to do with professional connections among academics, the availability of resources, or political influences than with the discovery of consistent behaviour.[29]

Fourth, if these 79 projects are representative of the current pattern of social research, then current practice tends to perpetuate the very characteristics that have prevented the scientific legitimisation of the social sciences. The 79 projects indicate the research practices young social scientists are being trained to follow and the direction that they are likely to take in their future scholarship. These studies also reflect what senior social researchers consider to be exemplars of social inquiry, while they serve as mentors to young scholars, endorse their efforts, and recommend them for academic positions. If such practices continue to be regarded as acceptable, social research will continue to generate results that are seen as superficial and having a limited range of applicability.

19

In addition to the unrestricted and superficial adherence of social studies to existing theories and the failure first to verify the selected theories, the proposals exhibit another interesting phenomenon. This is an excessive indulgence in the formality of methods,[30] an imbalance between procedures and objectives in favour of the former. Social science research should be directed toward recognising consistent patterns in a social system, describing those consistencies with the best possible formal representation, and then evaluating the accuracy of the representation. The choice of method for achieving this goal does not determine the accuracy of the representation. However, to achieve this goal, it is necessary to acquire the best empirical information about a system. Methods would be selected according to this data gathering and analysis criterion.

Fifth, the social sciences have adopted many technical terms from the natural sciences without consistent adherence to their original definitions, often creating meanings which are different from the original definitions. The social sciences tend to retain the general meaning of a term as it was originally defined in the natural sciences with slight modification when referring to elements appropriate to the social sciences. To the original meaning are added alternative meanings unique to the social sciences. Consider the term 'theory' itself. In the natural sciences the term generally means a formal explanatory summary of empirical information about various phenomena in a systematic, accurate, and consistent manner that enables testable predictions. In the social sciences, 'theory' may also refer to a system of thought about a subject area in the way that researchers subscribe to a school of thought, or philosophy. Social science theory may also possess the characteristic of prescribing conduct or influencing the very subject matter of which it is supposed to be an explanation, perhaps especially so in socio-political and economic theory.[31]

The above overview of the general state of the social sciences intends to disclose (1) that premature establishment of social science theories prevents their scientific advance, and (2) that the uncritical acceptance of existing theories may continue to prevent their significant development. In the following sections of this study, these two points will be clarified further through a comparison of the characteristics of the social sciences with those of the natural sciences. The social sciences' potential to become more scientific will be critically assessed, especially in relation to how that potential might be realised in time to meet the challenges of the social problems of the twenty-first century.

CHAPTER 3

THE SOCIAL SCIENCES AND NATURAL SCIENCES

Scholars have produced various analyses and comparisons of the social sciences with the natural sciences[32] For example, a general attempt was made by Ernest Gellner and the result presented in a tabular form.[33] Characteristics of the two systems of inquiry labelled 'science' are described and contrasted. His review concludes that the social sciences have failed to achieve the standards set by the natural sciences, lacking such attributes of the natural sciences as cumulativeness, testability, transcultural quality, and suggests that the 'social sciences' should more appropriately be called 'social thought.'

It is necessary to understand thoroughly the attributes of the social sciences so as to accurately assess their scientific potentiality. The present study represents an effort rigorously to examine the two systems of inquiry, those of the social sciences and those of the natural sciences, with regard to their objectives, their research approaches and procedures, and the special qualities inherent in their subject matter. Since both systems include a number of disciplines,[34] this discussion will necessarily be wider as it attempts to understand the characteristics of scientific inquiry that are essential to all endeavours claiming scientific status. Illustrations are provided.

First, with strong problem-solving expectations placed on them, the social scientists generally have pragmatic objectives. Social science theories and their applications are thought to be useful in explaining problems in society, predicting changes, guiding development, avoiding disasters, and enhancing the quality of life. Social scientists are of course interested in discovering causal relationships within various social phenomena, which will enable them to exert some control over the human condition. Attempts to unravel these causal connections usually come up against obstructions built into the instability of society, such as when having to deal with purposive behaviour. Even so social scientists at least strive to obtain insights about how and why social situations evolve, occasionally with insights resulting in other than causal explanations. This uncertainty encountered in the social sciences arises from the nature of their subject matter, the fact that they are concerned with human traits and activities, institutions (whether deliberately planned or not), and the existing social environment, none of which can be described as stable. Problems arise when the two science approaches confront each other. Politicians, steeped in social science traditions attempting to keep to a particular economic path, may face the dilemma whether to divulge or not the findings of natural science, for example health risks to the public, and how to act upon them.

The natural sciences, on the other hand, concentrate on the general principles of causation in the natural world. They are concerned with scientific truth, explaining the particulars by 'laws' that express the natural properties and relationships of matter and motion and the natural structure and dynamics of biological things. As a consequence of its basic nature, the subject matter of natural science, not being concerned with the non-physiological and non-physical human element, can be experimentally controlled during investigation, or at least a natural constancy can be recognised through obtaining a sufficient number of systematic observations, as in astronomy.

Second, regarding the process of theory construction, theories in the social sciences are based mainly on the unique experiences of the inquirers, and are the product of specific socio-cultural environments. Social theories are bound by space and time, which limit their applicability and predictive power. The applicability of social theory being confined to a particular socio-cultural environment, which gave rise to the theory in the first place, means that the theory cannot be entirely disproved, because the entities and relations expressed by it are of sufficient specificity to that environment to render generalisation and application in other settings inappropriate. In other words, the founders of theories in social science often culturally embed them, either intentionally or unintentionally, in the research language and interpretive structure of the environment in which the original developmental research was conducted. Hence, the theory is accessible only to those researchers familiar with the language and ways of thinking intrinsic to the culture of that environment. When a social theory is applied to a different socio-cultural setting, its relevance and appropriateness become problematic, for example as argued with reference to Kohlberg's stage theory of moral development. It is virtually impossible to repeat the same experiments in different conditions. As the human condition constantly changes, social research faces a further problem: how to identify invariances in human activities and how to study them scientifically. Because such in-

23

variances are difficult to identify, it is difficult in consequence to establish a firm empirical base for social science research.

It is always valuable, however, to understand the cultural and historical context of a theory, whether in political economy or in psychology, for example by studying the propounder's life.[35] The rare personal chemistry between Marx and Engels contributed much to the confident delivery of their version of class conflict, with Marx putting forward the theory in the academic surroundings of the British Museum Reading Room after receiving Engels' personal observations of working class conditions in the industrial Yorkshire city of Bradford. In jurisprudence too, it is essential to set a theoretical construct concerning the philosophy of law within its author's background. Here the recent example of Kenneth Starr, the presenter in President Clinton's impeachment trial can be quoted. It has been claimed that the zealous pursuit of the case by Starr was in no small measure due to his confidence in his own moral rectitude acquired as the son of a Fundamentalist preacher in South Texas, what he came to call 'the importance of institutions' and the role of law in upholding them.

The natural sciences, which have been used to serve as scientific prototypes for the social sciences, are paradoxically just the opposite. Natural science theories usually explain the relationship and existence of various empirically recognised and delimited objects and relations. They are formulated in a predictive manner, that is, they claim that if X occurs then Y should happen, given appropriate qualifying conditions, and in such a way that allows them to be challenged, validated, or disproved. A point may be reached where the recorded empirical evi-

24

dence contains too many inconsistencies and discrepancies between the evidence and the predictions; then the theory is abandoned as unscientific. Thus in the natural sciences theories usually succeed in identifying invariances, both constant properties and dynamic invariances,[36] which the social sciences cannot deliver, for example in the case of operant behaviourism.

That the natural sciences are considered superior to the social sciences is mainly due to the process of self-imposed evaluation and verification and constant scrutiny by fellow scientists who communicate with one another using the same technical language of the field, a practice that the social sciences have not been able to follow. Natural science needs evidence or proof for the establishment of a theory or result,[37] whereas in the social sciences it is rare to find an issue on which there is evidential consensus. In the natural sciences, laws and theories are usually built on empirical and experimental grounds, preceded by an initial stage of observation, imagination, and even speculation on the part of the inquirers. Invariances, in the form of constant physical properties of matter and natural laws, identified in the empirical world constitute the fundamental properties of the physical world.[38] It is assumed that once all or most of the parameters and variables related to certain invariances have been sorted out, it should be possible to offer explanations of almost everything based on them. Such a desire is the motivation for the endeavour to develop a unified theory. The intellectual pursuit of science is always to extend or adapt the current model to cover ever more classes of phenomena. As against that, social science will claim the existing theory applies to more individuals without putting it to the test.

25

In an attempt to be more scientific, the social sciences also construct theories upon certain empirical foundations. However, because of the nature of the subject matter, the empirical data that can be obtained in social studies are limited: they are likely to be experiential rather than experimental, superficial rather than profound, and they are temporally and culturally relative. As invariances are difficult, if not impossible, to identify, it is difficult to test and refine a social science theory. It is possible to rely only on the theory's perceptive quality rather than its scientific authoritativeness, as in the case of Freudian psychoanalysis, which has been used extensively as the foundation for many social inquiries.[39]

In consequence, social science theories are invested with special insights into specific social phenomena and complete their course of development relatively quickly within one or two generations. When older theories fail to keep up with changes, and lose their ability to describe new situations, they become outdated and are replaced by new theories. Usually older theories exert little, if any, direct cumulative effect on newer theories. Rather they are similar to a pendulum, taking contrary positions on certain key phenomena. Thus, social science theories have strong individualistic characteristics, they are associated with their main author, receive little outside input once the ideological position has been established, and in their short life span are basically self-sufficient from the beginning to the end.

By contrast, natural science theories, despite their being formulated by individual human effort, soon become an open and continuous process of objective inquiry, receiving challenges, absorbing new contributions and becoming more refined and mature, sounder, and more

26

powerful. The theory can then become dissociated from the personality of the original investigator, though it may retain his name. The following diagrams (Figures 1 and 2) show how differently social science and natural science theories evolve and develop.

The first diagram (Figure 1) illustrates the individualistic and dispersive type of development of the social sciences, in contrast with the cumulative and continuous, rocket type of development of the natural sciences.

Figure 1 depicts the dispersive character of theory development in the social sciences. The largest circles in the diagram represent the original formation of a theory by the founding theorist (e.g. Piaget, Skinner, and Kohlberg). The three sets of large circles with their associated smaller circles indicate that a number of approaches or theories linked to the same phenomenon may be pursued and developed simultaneously. These original theories are usually creative and insightful and, in consequence, tend to attract much attention from other scholars. Students of the founding theorists may become disciples of the theorists and never question the legitimacy of the theories but simply apply the theories to more and more cases. Other disciples may take issue with some aspect of the original theory and begin to generate a new formulation for that aspect, while still keeping the core of the original theory intact (represented by the smaller circles). Some may simply apply the theory to a different area of research altogether or to a different cultural setting and modify the specifications of the theory accordingly. These new theories are usually minor revisions of the original but a few could formulate major changes generating a 'neo-ism' (shaded circles). These second generation disciples and theories are represented by the

27

THE SCIENTIFIC MERIT OF THE SOCIAL SCIENCES

28

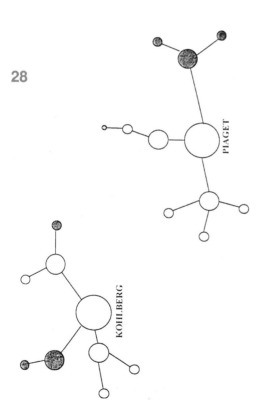

Legend:

○ Extension and proliferation of the original theory suggesting generations of the tradition

◉ Extension of the original theory with revision and reinterpretation which may appear in the form of a "neo-ism"

Figure 1: Dispersion Effect in the Social Sciences

next largest circles with the lines coming from the original theory representing the dependence of the second generation on the original. These second-generation theories may also attract attention and produce a third generation of theories which may in turn even produce a fourth. Each generation becomes increasingly less important (smaller circles) because a number of competing revisions have become available. These revisions with their own variations on the original theory and subsequent revisions provide different explanations of some aspect of the phenomenon of interest in the original theory. As time progresses and social and environmental, for example economic or political, characteristics change, which may trigger off changes in the theories, the original theory may become less relevant, though it may still be applied as if it realistically represented the new conditions. This is so despite the fact that the theory should no longer be of interest except in historical research. This representation prompts the use of the simile of branching bushes with the original theories as the roots of each bush and the disciples' revisions as the branches. In this kind of dispersive and individualistic development it may simply be by accident, coincidence, or pure chance that a theorist can devise a good explanation of a particular phenomenon.

29

The second diagram (Figure 2) illustrates an explosion, rocket-analogy rendering of the development of theories in the natural sciences, where the stages of the rocket lift-off are represented by **A, B, C**... In this conception scientific inquiry begins with the formulation of a theory or framework (A_0) that may not but usually does depend on earlier research. This theory could be a new interpretation of previous information or arise from original

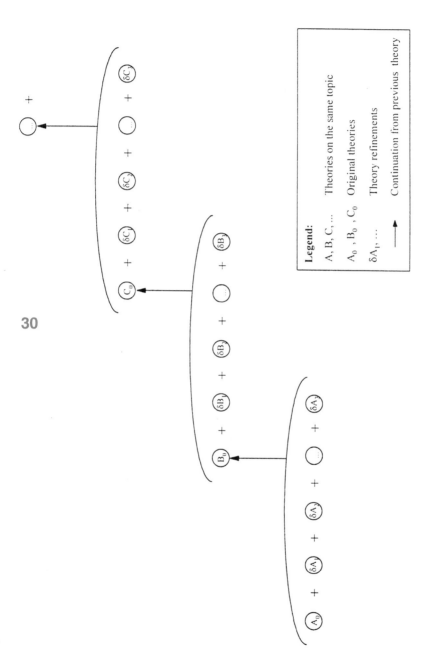

Figure 2: Continuative Pattern of Natural Science

ideas arrived at after an event newly observed. Based on the assumption of the 'truth' of this theory an evidential data record begins to accumulate which may at first suggest only small changes (δ) to the theory (e.g. increases in the accuracy of measurements or peripheral changes) but soon may require extensions (δA_1, δA_2, etc.) of the theory (e.g. formulation of qualifying rules, accounting for anomalies) creating a 'theoretical record' ($A_0 + \delta A_1 + \delta A_2 + \dots$). At some point in the inquiry its approach under the theoretical record (As) may have accumulated sufficient information to suggest a completely new approach to understanding the evidential record. A new theory (B_0) which reformulates the theoretical record (As) based on explaining new developments (e.g. in instrumentation, application in other fields, etc.) as well as discrepancies and inconsistencies that have arisen between the accumulated evidential record and the original theoretical record (As) then becomes the new basis for conducting inquiry. Research conducted under this reformulated theory adds to the evidential record and begins to change (δB_0) and to extend (δB_1, δB_2, etc.) the theory in turn generating its own theoretical record ($B_0 + \delta B_1 + \delta B_2 + \dots$). New developments and discrepancies and inconsistencies between the evidential and theoretical record (Bs) may again require the formulation of a new theory (Co) which again adds to the evidential record and generates a theoretical record ($Co + \delta C_1 + \delta C_2 + \dots$). This process may continue *ad infinitum* or until the theory so closely matches the empirical world that any additional changes will be merely cosmetic.

31

Each new stage (**B**, **C**, etc.) may not necessarily totally supplant the former stage. The 'outdated' theories may continue to be more appropriate and acceptable approxi-

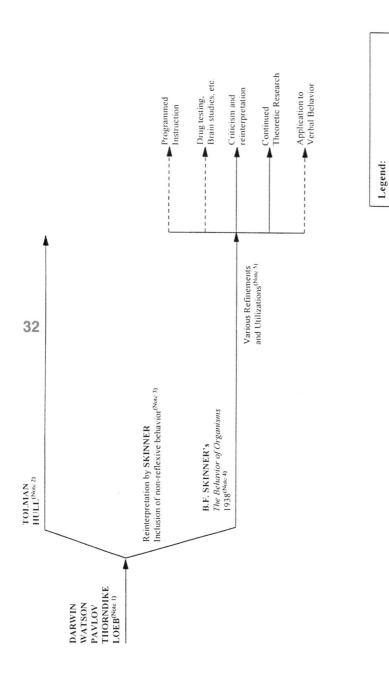

Figure 3: Culminate Development of Operant Behaviourism

mations within the context in which they were first developed and consequently utilised. Hence, inquiry in these earlier stages may continue because they provide a simpler and sufficient approximation within a limited context of application (δA_a, δB_a, etc.). It is not that the earlier stages were incorrect; rather, improved accuracy in measurement and observation require a more precise account of the evidence. The less refined stages may be used as tools for an immediate problem because they offer a simplified picture, making the problem easier to solve, while the subsequent stages can be interpreted as layers of refinement giving better approximations. For example, quantum mechanics would be considered a refinement of Newtonian mechanics, but a builder does not consider quantum mechanics when building a house. What has happened is that the main focus of research has shifted to the more refined stage, to quantum mechanics rather than Newtonian mechanics. Each stage should improve upon the predictive and/or explanatory power of the preceding theoretical record.

33

The third and fourth diagrams (Figures 3 and 4) provide more specific illustrations. The third diagram (Figure 3) depicts the development of the operant behaviourism of B.F. Skinner. Much of the text of the following explanation has been taken from comments describing the development of behaviourism made by Skinner himself.[40] Behaviourism originated as a response to the Darwinian 'revolution' in biology; an attempt to make the study of behaviour based on the observable responses and manipulable elements of an organism's environment (Note 1 in Figure 3). Charles Darwin himself contended that internal processes, choice and volition, contributed to determining what an animal did or did not do. Lloyd Morgan,

34

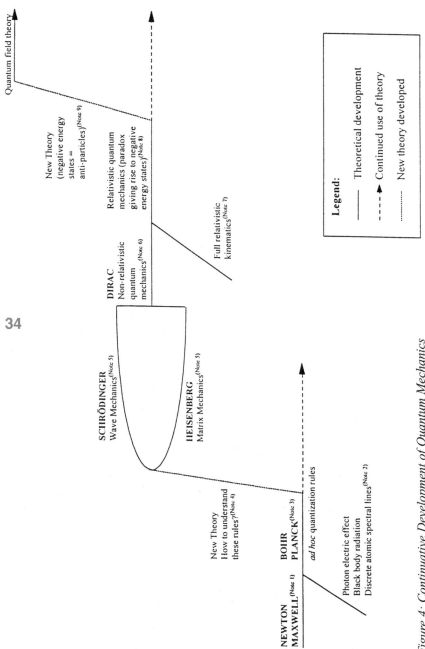

Figure 4: Continuative Development of Quantum Mechanics

the comparative psychologist and psychological philosopher, objected to these speculations and countered that
alternative explanations could be presented. John B.
Watson, the founder of behaviourism, took the next steps
by generalising that human behaviour could be accounted
for by explanations of external stimuli. With the acceptance of this assertion, an early variety of behaviourism
began to take shape. Watson began by investigating
instincts but later turned to conditioned reflexes, and his
associate Karl S. Lashley went even further into the
nervous system for explanations of behaviour.

Behaviourist research in the conditioned reflex tradition
did not end when Skinner began formulating his operant
form of behaviourism. In fact, Skinner's thesis, 'The
Concept of the Reflex in the Description of Behavior',
was in this tradition but was additionally influenced by
the work of physiologists like Jacques Loeb, philosophers
like Percy W. Bridgman and Bertrand Russell, arid controlled experiments such as those initiated by the Russian
physiologist and psychologist Ivan Pavlov. Other behaviourists, such as Edwin R. Guthrie, Clark L. Hull, and
Edward C. Tolman also formulated neobehaviourist
theories (Note 2 in Figure 3).

35

Skinner recognised that responses were only a small part
of the behaviour of complex organisms (Note 3 in Figure
3). The environment not only elicits behaviour from an
organism, it also selects forms of behaviour. The consequences of a behaviour in this sense become more
important than the antecedents or stimulants of
behaviour. Edward L. Thorndike was the first to study the
effects of consequences experimentally, but his investigation lacked the rigorous control Skinner desired. It also
attributed affective behaviour to internal processes.

Hence, Skinner undertook research on the selection of forms of behaviour by the environment which culminated in the development of a neobehaviourist system.

Skinner collected his investigations on the effects of complex contingencies of reinforcement in his book *The Behavior of Organisms* (Note 4 in Figure 3). This work represents the culmination of Skinner's research into a framework for the investigation of behaviour, that is, a variant of behaviourism called operant behaviourism. The philosophy and techniques described in the book have remained essentially unchanged over the years, although the sophistication of the apparatus has improved and the scope of application has broadened as a result. While later studies may have made refinements, none changed Skinner's ideas on the development of operant behaviourism as expounded in *The Behavior of Organisms* in any significant way.

Operant behaviourists continued to do basic research, but their work tended to widen the scope of applicability rather than test its own foundations (Note 5, represented by the dashed lines). Many of these experiments studied more complex contingencies of reinforcement using non-human organisms although some studies and applications such as programmed instruction were conducted with humans. Other applications were studies testing the effect of drug-taking on behaviour and studies of factory workers. Skinner and others speculated about the universal applicability of behavioural techniques to investigating behaviour and shaping the social environment (e.g. Skinner's utopian ideas, in *Walden Two*; 'Selection of Consequences', and *Beyond Freedom and Dignity*.

New interpretations and research programs were developed as a response to Skinner's ideas (Note 5 in Figure 3, represented by solid lines). Some of these may have been other neobehaviouristic systems such as Edward C. Tolman's 'purposive behaviourism' and Clark L. Hull's 'hypothetical deductive' system brought to the forefront by contrasting their ideas against Skinner's.

Skinner's name had become synonymous with operant behavioural research, and evoking his name whether in support of his research or its rejection brought attention until Chomsky's formulation of transformational grammar in his *Syntactic Structures* began, arguably, the relegation of Skinner to history. This theory is in turn being revised with linguists such as Clahsen[41] attaching an increasing importance to the reinforcing role of the speech input of the tutor or exchange partner as part of language development.

37

Figure 4 represents the development of quantum theory. The development of the theory began with a pre-established theory that described what was at the time accepted and known to be true of the empirical world. The development of quantum physics had as a jumping-off point the ideas and laws formulated by Isaac Newton and James Clerk Maxwell and others who built upon their work (Note 1 in Figure 4).

As investigation into multi-layered, complex phenomena progressed, effects were observed that were incapable of explanation by the application of the Newton-Maxwell theories. Such anomalies as the photon electric effect, black body radiation, and discrete atomic spectral lines defied explanation through the macro-level laws of Newton and Maxwell. However, the Newton-Maxwell theories were not shown to be wrong. They were sufficiently accurate in their context (that of macro-level observation), although unable to describe or predict micro-level phenomena (Note 2 in Figure 4).

At this point physicists Niels Bohr and Max Planck began to create *ad hoc* quantisation rules that made a start with accounting for the discrepancies and inconsistencies that had begun to accumulate in the evidential data. These *ad hoc* quantisation rules were the beginning of quantum mechanics, because they decreed that certain quantities could assume only discrete values. In particular, transitions could happen only in discrete steps (quanta). The *ad hoc* quantisation rules gave physicists a physically intuitive picture of what actually was going on (Note 3 in Figure 4).

It became apparent that the Newton-Maxwell formalisation was not sufficient for explaining micro-level phenomena, unable, for example, to explain the almost instantaneous emission of photons when light shines on a metallic surface. Also, theory and experiment do not agree about the distribution of energy for each frequency of light in a black body. Nevertheless, the Newton-Maxwell theory was and is still useful. In macroscopic cases (e.g. when constructing a building or a bridge), quantum effects are averaged out, because many quanta are involved. This averaging out does not mean that quantum effects are not happening (atoms are still held together by forces described by quantum mechanics), it is just that it is impossible to directly measure the effects of each quantum. The Newton-Maxwell theory did not die with the development of quantum mechanics (illustrated by the continuation arrow in the diagram), though it ceased being the most accurate representation of what happens in the world. Given the *ad hoc* quantisation rules, physicists began to try to formalise these rules into a coherent theory (Note 4 in Figure 4, represented by the dotted vertical line).

It was left to two physicists to develop formalisations of the *ad hoc* rules of quantisation. Werner Heisenberg developed a mathematical representation based on matrix theory, termed matrix mechanics. Erwin Schrödinger formalised the rules into wave mechanics. Theirs were two mathematical interpretations of the same physical system, quantum mechanics, and based on the same data record (Note 5 in Figure 4).

The two mathematical formalisations of Heisenberg and Schrödinger were believed to be equivalent by being derived from the study of the same physical system (i.e. the same evidence). It was Paul Adrien Maurice Dirac who showed mathematically that the wave and matrix interpretations of quantum mechanics were equivalent, i.e. both interpretations were correct, though they were different representations. Recognition of this equivalence brought together the two interpretive camps under what became known as non-relativistic quantum mechanics (Note 6 in Figure 4). It was here that difficulties were encountered such as those that appeared when physicists attempted to take into account relativistic kinematics. Negative energy states were inevitable. They defied past experience. Furthermore, the agreement with experiments was incomplete (Note 7 in Figure 4).

Again it was Dirac who turned out as one of the principal architects in the merging of non-relativistic quantum mechanics with full relativistic kinematics into relativistic quantum mechanics, inventing a new equation which

39

makes the spin of an electron (half integer) come out naturally. It was a branch of mathematics (spinors) few physicists knew about. However, the same paradox reappears when Dirac's equation is accepted. This is because it gives rise to negative energy states (Note 8 in Figure 4).

The paradox of negative energy states needed to be resolved. The resolution came in the form of a new interpretation which associates the negative energy states as anti-particles, so that their negative energies are made positive. To incorporate this property, that is, to have a natural mathematical structure for its formulation, quantum field theory was proposed, whereby creation and annihilation of particles and anti-particles became a part of the theory. The relativistic quantum mechanics formalisation remained and remains a useful theory when dealing with a micro-level elementary process at low energy levels, for instance, if one is not concerned with particle creation or annihilation. It is also useful as the lowest order approximation (regarding energy) in looking for relativistic effects.[42] As evidential data continue to accumulate, quantum field theory may in turn be replaced as the most accurate and accepted representation of how the world works. For now it is the best theory under which to conduct research in quantum physics (Note 9 in Figure 4), although there are mathematical difficulties that remain to be resolved.

Because of the constancy of the subject matter, the identifiability of invariances, the advancement of experimental methods and procedures, the range and scope of researchable areas can all be clearly understood and the agenda intelligently determined as a result. The study of the natural sciences has been analogous to charting a map, fitting a jigsaw puzzle, or going through a filtering and purification process. It is intellectually progressive and certain. As against that, social scientists are likened to blind men who try to figure out what animal an elephant is by touching a certain part of it. They all obtain some concrete experience of the animal and somehow believe they can determine the nature of the whole beast from their individual and restricted vantage points.

41

CHAPTER 4

REDIRECTION OF THE SOCIAL SCIENCES

That the social sciences, while flourishing as academic disciplines and professional programmes, are far from being scientific at the present stage of development is evident. Since scientific inquiry, in the natural science sense, is a search for truth, the continuing trend in the social sciences of uncritical adherence to 'big-name' theories and the popularity of 'methodology' are both opponents rather than proponents of their scientific legitimisation. Do social scientists really want to see their 'sciences' evolve into other types of 'science' which have abandoned their original chosen model, that of the rational, objective, and experimental form of inquiry demonstrated by the natural sciences? If this is going to be the future of the social sciences, then new definitions for the term science and related concepts will have to be created. A different expectation of what the social sciences can accomplish will have to be formulated, as the social sciences give up their claim of being scientific in the traditional sense. No doubt, the laxity of *some* scientific requirements and the freedom and variety of approaches will promote many imaginative and colourful investigations, which may manifest wisdom and insight, but since they cannot be verified, will remain inconclusive.

The original goal of transforming social inquiry into a strong science by providing it with an empirical basis and experimental methods may still be the wish of many social scientists. If so, then the problem confronting the social sciences is how to redirect efforts toward their becoming a stronger science, or even a fully developed exact science. However, before this topic can be considered, it is necessary to answer a series of crucial questions: Do the social sciences possess the potentiality of becoming exact sciences? In other words, can they fulfil the necessary criteria, as the natural sciences generally are tested to do, for being truly scientific? Will social scientists be able to generate research that will assist in the recognition of important systems operating in the social environment? Can they design research that will be able to recognise the regular patterns of behaviour at work in these systems? Can they design research that will assist in the identification of important human and social variables and parameters within these systems? In other words: will social scientists be able to recognise the exact relationships that exist among these variables and parameters and their relations to entities outside the systems? More importantly, will social scientists be able to identify the constant properties and invariant dynamics at work in these systems? This assumes their willingness and ability to overcome the cultural relativity of current social science research.[43]

Whether the social sciences can become fully developed sciences like the natural sciences depends on whether researchers can identify, locate, and study the invariances in human traits and activities. This comes down to two fundamental questions, as Gellner puts them: 'Is there but one kind of man, or are there many? Is there but one world, or are there many?'[44]

The answer to one of these questions does not presuppose the answer to the other. Evidence obtained from scientific inquiries into the physical universe has led to the conclusion that there can be but one physical world and one truth about it, and not many. However, the 'oneness' of mankind is a separate question. The existence of various cultural traditions and the exhibition of different individual aptitudes have led to the belief that there are indeed many different kinds of human beings, and even to give out that some are superior and some inferior, inhabiting 'different worlds'. Errors in the perception of human phenomena, because of their elusiveness, have complicated the problem further.

If there are different kinds of human beings (other than men and women) and if they are fundamentally different from one another, then the likelihood of the social sciences succeeding in their attempt to establish a generalising study of humans which would come up with comprehensive and accurate theories about them and their societies is small. Indeed the problem has to be put more reflectively: that is, while using criteria to discover differences, it is also possible to notice similarities. Human beings everywhere share the identical fundamental structure of molecules; all have the same neural system that makes up their cerebral structure; and all grow in experience in the same way. These common features which set limits to physical and mental behaviour are derived from a common human genetic makeup. While one individual may appear different from another because each possesses unique genetic material, the processes that determine how that genetic material functions to produce each one are the same. Even though each individual accumulates different life experiences,

45

the fundamental physical interpretive faculties for understanding these experiences (i.e. the brain and how it functions) are essentially the same for everyone. All human beings are both different and at the same time similar to one another. The differences are superficial and are largely developed through generations of accommodation and adaptation to the environment; the similarities are more fundamental, being the characteristics of a common human nature. In this sense, all human beings may be said to belong to one single kind. There is only one human species designated by that name. While the many strains of that same species may exhibit different arrangements of the basic building blocks of human beings, the building blocks themselves are identical.

These findings did not stop the controversy surrounding the different results obtained in IQ tests conducted with persons of different races and traced to hereditary factors from being exaggerated by some social scientists who claim the existence of a genetically different human intelligence which requires more reaction time to respond to stimuli.[45] Particularly dangerous were the uncontrolled and incomplete observations of human achievement by social anthropologist philosophers, such as Houston Stewart Chamberlain, who, proceeding from developments in the nineteenth century, concluded that race influenced human personality and behaviour. Chamberlain's work led, going beyond membership of a social class to racial origins, from claims of racial superiority to incitement to racial hatred made by the Nazi ideologue, Alfred Rosenberg, in his *Der Mythus des 20. Jahrhunderts* in a significant reference to the twentieth century in the title of his book.

Chemistry tells us that diamonds and charcoal have many distinct properties, although they are both made of carbon molecules. The study of social science observes the behaviour of human beings both as individuals and collectively. These collective phenomena can be very different, because of the numerous aspects they can assume, from individual ones.

The implications are that human traits and behaviour, and perhaps even human thought, can eventually be studied scientifically, particularly through the collaboration of biological and social research. An optimistic view predicts that if the genetic makeup of individuals were fully understood, scientists 'could assess the risk of disease years before the first symptoms appeared, identify a criminal from a single hair, and uncover the mysteries of how we think, grow, heal, and age'.[46] Successful decoding of the 80.000 human genes will enable researchers to develop drugs and other treatments tailored to an individual specific genetic profile. As the well known US Government funded Genome Project, which has been pursuing an exhaustive investigation of the genetic makeup of the human race, moves along, scientists may have reason to be cautiously optimistic.[47]

Even if transforming the social sciences into a fully developed exact science takes a long time to accomplish, it is time to start working toward that goal by removing the three obstacles which delay it. These are the uncritical attachment to and use of popular theories, what may be called guru worship, the entrapment of methodology, discussed in Chapter Three of this study, as well as the purposive procedures used by less cautious social researchers who abandon the scientific approach in their investigations. The following five measures, which

47

adhere to the generally accepted principles of science, are considered essential to promote the scientific advancement of the social sciences, making them more like natural sciences while retaining their distinctive areas of concern and methodology. Subjected to these tests some social sciences are more likely to make the grade than others.

(I) Clarification of terms and terminology. An agreed, common vocabulary, as in the natural sciences, is absolutely essential if there is to be any advance in the social sciences. They   must free themselves from ambiguity and confusion. The misunderstanding of Platonic and Aristotelian terms has dogged the West. The concept behind the Confucian principle of 'Rectification of Names' is the key. Confucius said: 'If names are not rectified, then language will not be in accord with truth. If language is not in accord with truth, then things cannot be accomplished'[48] Economics, particularly in its post-Marshallian form, is in danger of losing its credibility as a result of the ambiguity and loose nature of its preferred terminology. The deliberate vagueness of much educational theory gives credence to the complaints of practising educationists that looseness in the use of words indicates a looseness in thought. The overused in-words 'free market', multicultural' and intercultural education' provide an illustration.

Certain key terms in social science research, such as the term 'theory' itself, also 'model', and 'principle', have not only been defined differently from their use in the natural sciences, but it is also a fact that different reference sources in the social sciences may define identical terms quite differently.[49] A mechanism, such as an editorial board, consisting of leading scholars from different social science areas, established to work on a special dictionary project to be sponsored by relevant academic bodies would develop general guidelines for the adoption, modification, and change of terms for the various divisions of the social sciences as well as for the field as a whole.[50] With unambiguous definitions of terms and concepts superfluous jargon could be eliminated, questionable, not thought-through, ideas could be weeded out, and social scientists could gradually develop a more consistent, concise, and precise communication system. This is the first prerequisite for any serious scientific research if it is to merit the name 'science.'

(II) Systematic investigation and assessment of important and popular theories in the social sciences. In the process of constructing a theoretical framework, theories need to be reviewed and scrutinised for their soundness and appropriateness before adoption and application. A comprehensive investigation into the background and origin, development, research design, generalisation and claim of universality, evaluation and application, and the influence of individual theories would be necessary to achieve this. A sample scheme has already been developed and has proved to be effective in such endeavour.[51]

49

The scheme was designed by the author as an instrument for guiding his graduate students at the University of Michigan to conduct background investigation of social and behavioural science theories. This was a prerequisite for the interpretation, use and adaptation of any theory in their research. This scheme of investigation consists of the nine following parts:

- finding out the theory founder's biological and intellectual background

- locating the theory founder's academic works and related writings

- examining works written about the founder of the theory

- assessing the influence of the theory during the theory founder's lifetime

- studying the approach and processes leading to the formation and establishment of the theory

- investigating the social and cultural environment in which the theory was developed

- finding out whether the founder of the theory ever claimed universal validity of the theory, which many theory followers take for granted

- finding out whether the theory has ever been empirically tested by the theory founder himself or by others. If it has been, what was the result of the tests

- finding out if the theory founder himself or others have ever given suggestions about how the theory might be used or tested. This scheme represents a serious approach to critically understand a social science theory. While it is comprehensive, it needs to be refined further.

(III) Comparison and confrontation of theories bearing on the same theme or problem. With terms clarified and communication barriers largely removed, with individual theories reviewed and their strengths and weaknesses understood, those theories which have contributed to accepted relevant topics can be selected, matched and compared. A 'confrontation' of 'theories' can allow social scientists of different schools of thought to meet, discuss, argue, debate, study with one another, and escape from the confines of their own theoretical traditions. In this way the necessary condition for productive scientific communication can be established. Relevant research findings obtained through different approaches and interpreted from different perspectives can be freed from misrepresentation, allowing the theoretical counterparts to object with reason or to assent with understanding. Conflicting theories may find points of mutual agreement, which in turn may become the loci for collaborative, further investigations of the topic. Indeed, carefully and intelligently designed comparison and challenge of social science research may not only lead to the formation of a new basis for theoretical development, but also foster the arrival of a genuine community of social scientists, in which participants can involve themselves in the pursuit of scientific excellence free from academic biases and ideological and political influences.[52] The crucial question is who is to decide on the criteria.

The study of the role of the first language (mother tongue) in the acquisition of a second or foreign language can be suggested as another example of the problems associated with the establishment of psycho-social theory in view of the shifting data which becomes available as the study unfolds and the changing focus of emphasis.

If we take Clyne's widely received 1960's view of the process of language transfer and its effect as the starting point then this has been significantly modified so as to leave the role of the transfer or interference much reduced. It is now accepted to being responsible for

51

learners using certain constructions in the second language which are 'incorrect' in that language and which affect the formal properties in language learning. Transfer is absent in language development which is activated with the use of communicative skills and language behaviour. This takes place independently in all language systems. Indeed, Pit Corder suggests that no firm conclusion for language teaching can arise from a better understanding of the role of the mother tongue in second language learning since the processes of language use are neither conscious nor available to introspection.

In other words, while the learning process itself can be influenced by the use of some mother tongue structures in the second language, as the latter becomes more fluent it develops independently from the former and can resort to deliberate borrowings from it or indeed from another language altogether.

The acceptance of one or the other transfer theory thus hinges on the emphasis given to the cognitive (learning) or the communicative fluency (behaviour) study of the process of second language acquisition.[53] Including the affective dimension in the process which can determine its speed, what with learners actually wanting or not wanting to learn another language, would make the setting up of another social science 'certainty' more problematic. Empirical evidence is controversial because of the fact that second language knowledge stems from three sources: language universals as well as mother tongue and the target (second) language.

(IV) Surveying extensively the range and scope of human problems to obtain a vision of the whole picture enabling a comprehensive agenda for inquiry to

be designed, and solutions reviewed and adjusted periodically. The interconnectedness of various problems, issues and topics has to be understood so as to make it possible to identify the appropriate, specific items for investigation. While the topics chosen for the study should be small enough to be controllable, the study itself should be substantial enough to be significant to accommodate understanding the topic itself as well as to allow planning the investigation of a larger area on the agenda. The eventual goal of social science is to work toward achieving as complete and accurate knowledge as is possible of human beings and their societies, while allowing for the fact that they may be different in detail and that the social science procedures themselves are liable to be tested at any time. This will require individual social researchers to appreciate the importance of communication and cooperation among fellow inquirers on a long-term basis; a daunting task judging from past experience. Through the continuous efforts of both the involved individuals and groups, information, insights, procedural techniques, and skills will gradually accumulate and be refined, enabling a scientific understanding of human society to emerge.

53

The part memory plays in the development of human learning and the impact of information stimuli have been differently evaluated affecting the role assigned to television on children's learning. The James Bulger murder committed in November 1993 in Bootle, England, by two 11 year old boys can be compared with the more recent Luk Chi case in 1998 Hong Kong involving a gang of adolescents four years older than the victim. In both cases the viewing of television gangster programmes by the juvenile perpetrators of the murders was quoted by some as a contributory factor inciting to the crimes committed. The court in Hong Kong heard that one of the members of the gang convicted inflicted blows on Luk while reading a poem inspired by the programme 'Teddy Boy', a view supported by the academic evidence provided by Dr Eric-Ma Kit Wai, a professor of journalism and communication in the University of Hong Kong. The psychological opinions of the causal relationship quoted were divided. The judge in the British case preferred not to bring in the factor of the impact of television viewing into his judgment, while 'violence in the media' was brought in by the defence in the Hong Kong trial. The 'confusion between fact and fiction presented as entertainment' makes it difficult to apply moral standards; the dismissal of a complaint against the 'Teddy Boy' programme took away a further plank of certainty.

54 **(V) Developing translation, transformation, and unified theories in the social sciences**. This insight evolved through the study of the development of quantum theory in modern physics. As discussed in the previous Chapter, Paul Dirac developed a mathematical proof that Schrödinger's wave mechanics was identical to the matrix mechanics of Heisenberg, that is, he developed a transformation theory that showed these two mechanics to be equivalent interpretations of the same non-relativistic quantum mechanics. In the social sciences, many 'theories' revolve around a certain topic, trying to interpret it with their own approaches and languages, often with limited resources and success. Thus Piaget, Skinner, and Kohlberg, all contemporaries, investigated how human beings learn. However, each studied learning, starting from a unique approach: Piaget used clinical observations of children in developing his stage theory of

mental development;[54] Skinner examined laboratory animals in developing his notion of contingencies of reinforcement and then applied these ideas to the learning environment, that is, learning as occurring through the formation of complex contingencies of reinforcement for children;[55] Kohlberg used interview procedures with socially privileged boys as the foundation for developing his stages of moral education.[56] Each of these theorists may be correct within his separate approaches. However, social science requires a mechanism for bringing together the results of the three perspectives and others like them into a comprehensive theory or framework. For such a mechanism to evolve researchers must be able to effectively communicate with and understand one another across their different approaches.

In the previous Chapter, an 'explosion' model of theory development was presented. Theory development as this model describes it may not be inappropriate for the social sciences. However, if the position is taken that a single unified theory about a system should be discoverable, then social science would require a rigorous mechanism that harnesses and directs the explosion into a rocket-like effort that homes in on such a unified theory. The several paragraphs that follow suggest a possible mechanism for achieving this end.

55

First, since a phenomenon may be investigated using several approaches, and from various perspectives within each approach, and since several theories may emerge from these approaches, a preliminary mechanism for effective communication among the diverse approaches is essential. As part of theory development in social science, researchers could formulate 'translation theories' that permitted them to understand one another despite using different approaches and theories with similar and differing meanings of terms.

A developed translation theory functions like a specialised dictionary where each term has only one meaning and terms which appear to have the same meaning are identified as to their precise meanings. Wherever required, translation theory would translate terms in one theory into terms in another theory. If more than one theory used the same term, it should be possible to determine whether in the context of each theory or approach the term does represent the same empirical or theoretical entity. If the term has an identical meaning or represents the same entity within each theory, the term should be standardised. If the meaning of the term differs within each theory, it should be necessary to distinguish between the different meanings within each theory and to reveal the differences by revising the term's meaning and creating new, more appropriate terms. If a theory claims to use a unique term, it would be possible to determine whether what the term represents has an alternative term used in other theories. If several terms are being used to represent the same empirical or theoretical entity, then after careful comparison one of the terms or a new term should be chosen as standard. If different terms represent unique entities, each term should become standard for what it represents.[57] A start could be made with the terms 'stage' and 'level of development' discussed in the Introductory Chapter of this study.

The assumption that different theories about the same phenomenon have discovered unique aspects of that phenomenon would prove a major stimulus for new research within the separate approaches to confirm the existence of the unique elements claimed. For instance, different terms may be used to refer to different degrees of specificity about an object or process requiring the identification of the different degrees in order to make it possible to differentiate between the terms used. Terms revealed as just different names for the same entity would be eliminated. Unambiguous and commensurable communication among scholars is a prerequisite for securing competent advancement in scientific research. To be sure, the description of this process makes it seem more straightforward than it will turn out in practice, the immediate problem being the selection of samples.

Second, after the translation theory has been adopted, it will be necessary to proceed to formulate 'transformation theories.' To understand the specification of a transformation theory, let us suppose that there are two theories about the same phenomenon, Theory X and Theory Y. The transformation theory turns the theoretical entities and processes and, to the extent that models are concerned, the empirical entities and processes of Theory X, into the relevant entities and processes of Theory Y. It would be desirable that every entity and process of Theory X coincided with one and only one entity or process of Theory Y and conversely that each entity or process of Theory Y had an entity or process in Theory X that coincided with it (an isomorphism). A one-to-one relation-preserving match (i.e. a homomorphism) would probably be sufficient.

Naturally, two such ideal types of matchings will occur infrequently since conceptual entities in one theory may have many manifestations in another. However, as a result of the transformation theory not only could researchers communicate using the same language but they could transform their theory into another theory that may be a

57

more appropriate specification for the particular situation being researched. If we confine ourselves to the disciplines quoted earlier an investigation of the educational implications of intelligence development under certain conditions would take comparative account of the differences actually measured.[58]

Third, once the transformation theory has been developed, the procedures that have evolved will enable researchers to formulate a single unified theory about the phenomenon which the different individual theories attempted to explain. The individual theories should not be dismissed, for within particular, smaller area applications they may give simpler, yet adequate, approximations of the system. Analogous to the continued use of Newtonian mechanics, social theories that have been supplanted by a more accurate approximation to the system will still be useful within the approach and environment in which they were originally formulated. These theories would reference the single theory as a foundation. Although social researchers may argue about just how to formulate translation, transformation, and unified theories, they must be able to agree that conducting such research and its subsequent success will significantly strengthen the knowledge base in the social sciences.

(VI) Sorting out and clearing the traps of method. Social scientists often consider 'scientific' research to be determined by the particular method employed in conducting it. No exclusive set of rules, or 'scientific method', exists that tells scientists exactly how or where to conduct their individual research. This individually initiated research depends entirely on the creativity of the researcher to devise the means for discovering or testing consistent patterns in a system. An informal process exists, however, requiring the rigorous establishment of results before acceptance by the research community. Adherence of most natural scientists to the same world view, that is, agreement on the important field advancing topics to investigate and how to investigate them, which had not always been the case, assists in this informal process.

As discussed in the Introductory Chapter, the social sciences lack an agreed world view and in consequence dispose of a weak informal process for deciding when supportive evidence legitimates acceptance of new results and when not. The following paragraphs discuss some aspects of the dynamics of research, namely, data collection, data analysis, and model and theory development. They also suggest some improvements that may help make social science results more valid. A proviso for this discussion is that social scientists can recognise what is researchable and what is not researchable within current limitations and strive toward attempting those parts that can be accomplished with a broader objective always within sight.[59]

59

Before discussing these aspects of research, a brief introductory description of the 'research dynamic' may be helpful. The most important part of research is the collection of relevant data. However, data collection is partially dependent on the identification of the important and relevant parameters and variables in a system. This identification in turn is partially dependent on the analysis of the limited data that do get collected even with an incomplete identification of parameters and variables. The analysis of the data may assist in specifying a more complete list of the parameters and variables requiring the collection of additional data. Hence, as simplistic as this description may be, it is possible to begin to see how research progresses by constant reference to the data and to prior information. Despite possible unidentified and misidentified parameters and variables, the attempted research can progress, based on the data analyses, to develop models and theories about the system. At this point researchers have the incentive to make the models and theories more accurate through the collection and analysis of additional data relevant to this objective.

This brief description reveals that research is not a linear process directed toward a single climactic objective. Rather, research is a complex recursive network containing many feedback loops whose function it is to reassess prior information in the light of current achievements. The dynamic elements of data collection, data analysis, and model and theory development with respect to social science research will now be examined.

Data collection in the social sciences faces some unique obstacles. Most unfortunate is the absence of mechanisms for identifying important and relevant parameters and variables in social systems. This difficulty is linked to another obstacle, which is the heterogeneity of the subject matter of the social sciences. Unlike electrons where every electron has the same characteristics as every other electron, human beings and the groups that they form do not possess homogeneous sets of characteristics. As a result, subjects are enlisted for experiments and numerical data collected under conditions that can never be fully replicated, using a process of sampling from some total group, or population. It is accepted that the most desirable sample is a random sample, a sample drawn from a population in such a way that every element of the population has an equal chance of being selected.

Given an adequate sample size, a true random sample is accepted as typically representative of the population which permits researchers to make inferences about the population based on analyses of the sample. However, rarely do social researchers ever obtain true random samples unless the area investigated is small enough to be fully covered by the samples made. Even so, social researchers are prone to produce inferences about the population investigated although the sample is representative only of some subgroup of the total. As mentioned earlier, Piaget studied only European children but claimed his results were representative of all children. Now, unless Piaget was investigating a basic universal characteristic of child growth, which would require a substantiation he did not provide, his inference was inappropriate. This example demonstrates the limitations of such investigations.

The inability of social researchers to collect data from an appropriate sample is largely influenced by factors external to the research proper, that is, funding, access, and time. Data collection is usually the most expensive part of a social research project which causes many social researchers to reduce data collection to the minimum required for deriving results from their study. Also, social researchers may have access to only a limited segment of the population of interest (due to geographic proximity, subject availability) while time constraints placed on the researcher may function to further degrade the data collection phase of research. As a result, researchers have often turned to a variety of readily available sources of data to use in their studies. These alternative sources include large government data sources (such as census data, tax data and other), private data collection agencies, and the findings of other researchers. The large-scale use of secondary data sources limits the researcher's freedom and control over deciding what data are important to collect and how to collect them. Hence, as a surrogate for the desired data, researchers must utilise the best approximations from the available data set. To the effect that analysis techniques and models and theories advance only as the level of detail and sophistication of the available data improves, this need of substitution has implications for the research enterprise and the accuracy of results that can be expected. As the most important phase of the research dynamics data collection is well worth the expense and time required to collect representative samples.

Since responsibility for defraying the expenses of a research project is affected by its perceived usefulness to the sponsor, the cost of sampling is a further factor in abandoning social science projects, or labelling them as less scientific before trying them out first. Unlike in the social sciences moral value judgements are not essential in the physical sciences, as argued by Scriven.[60] Conversely massive and indiscriminate data collection, where the aims decide the priorities of the inquiry, will not enable researchers to generate meaningful and valid results.

Another aspect of data collection has to do with the procedures used to acquire data. The traditional methods of collecting data in the social sciences include surveys, interviews, observations, ethnographic study, and testing. Once a preliminary target sample has been determined one of these procedures or possibly a number of them will be used to solicit information from subjects in the sample. Discussion of the strengths and weaknesses of these data collecting procedures for specific types of projects is beyond the scope of this study. Suffice it to say that the effective size and representativeness of the sample which a procedure can draw on, the depth and detail of the obtainable data, and the variety of analyses that can be performed on the data, constrain the appropriate use of each procedure.

Issues of calibration of data collection instruments are rarely deliberated in the social sciences. Calibration in natural science means that when a new or more accurate instrument is introduced that new instrument must be brought into agreement with established knowledge by repeating past experiments with it. Adjustments may have to be made to the instrument to make it agree closely with the experiments that produced the previous results. When adjustments fail to calibrate the instrument, natural scientists face a dilemma because they cannot readily decide whether the failure is the result of a bad instrument or whether the new instrument has revealed some flaw in previous theory. The social sciences have no mechanism for the calibration of new instruments against past theories. This deficiency may in part be due to the lack of a reliable knowledge base upon which to base the calibration process. However, a more significant reason is that in social research data collection instruments are often situationally designed, that is, social researchers design data collection instruments relative to the topic they are investigating and to the environment in which the study is being conducted. This lack of continuity and consistency in the data record that a process of calibration would resolve creates a major obstacle for the development of sound, reliable social theories.

63

Data analysis of collected data represents a further element of the research dynamics. For the types of data collected, social research analysis procedures are not necessarily wrong. However, the claims and conclusions that are often drawn from the analyses by social researchers are inappropriate for what the results can actually demonstrate. For instance, many statistical analyses are correlational, and correlation only specifies that a relationship exists between two entities without specifying its precise nature. However, some analysts, basing themselves on a correlational analysis, claim confirmation of a causal relationship. Now a *causal* relation between two entities is always the result of an interpretation made by the researcher based on observation of the system, speculation, or experience. Analyses do not locate a relation nor do they confirm that the relation is causal. Most analyses do not even identify a relation but only test what the researcher believes to be a relationship present in a system. In this sense most social analysis procedures are exploratory. This property is desirable because social scientists want to base models and theories on empirical data. However, through exploratory studies one would want to be able to recognise and differentiate significant parameters and variables and the relations among them. Hence, the challenge for social researchers is to improve their ability to recognise patterns.[61]

An important phase of the research dynamics is the development of abstract models and theories based upon what has been learned from the data analyses. Unfortunately, as mentioned earlier in this chapter, in the absence of hard empirical evidence social science often begins with conceptualising a model or theory of how social phenomena function. Such philosophising inter-

64

feres with the data collection and analysis processes because empirical data become secondary to and supportive
of the theory rather than providing the impetus for the
discovery of theory. Social researchers tend to prescribe
'theories' for the phenomena that they study. Regardless
of whether the prescribed 'theory' accurately represents a
phenomenon, human beings can modify their behaviour
in response to a 'theory', rendering that 'theory' no
longer useful.

Clearly, social theory has a number of obstacles that must
be overcome. A way in which these difficulties can be
overcome is by developing theories firmly based on
empirical research, and once the theory has been established, re-evaluating and improving the data collected
and analyses conducted to arrive at the theory. If theories
become obsolete because people change their behaviour
in response to their predictions, then social scientists
should learn from these experiences and return to the data
to locate parameters, variables, and relations basic
enough that will be invariant to the purposive behaviour
of people. It must be stressed that theory is not the end of
social research. Rather, theory is a new beginning, for
certainly the first attempt at theory will not be the most
accurate representation of the social phenomenon
studied.

65

**(VII) Recognising that social sciences are culturally
bound and studying the significance of cultural factors in the selection, application, and assessment of
social science theories and knowledge**. Existing social
science theories were largely constructed upon fashion-
able and superficial situations current at the time. By no
means are they non-spatial, non-temporal, and transcultural. When using them cross-culturally, unexpected

effects and side effects are likely to be produced. Arbitrary adoption and application of social theories, economic, educational, political, or other, may lead to inconclusive results, as happened in the Soviet Union, China, North Korea, and Cuba, when they embraced Marxism as their prescriptive theory for society building. Indeed, transfer, transplanting or borrowing of social theories and practices have to be made a systematic field for serious investigation, which would also be necessary to test to what extent the application has in fact kept to the original model.

(VIII) Use of social science theories as a test of their function and power. At this stage of development of the social sciences, it will be hard to verify a social theory in a strictly experimental and controlled way. The solution is to select 'promising' social science theories, apply them carefully, and evaluate the consequences, bearing in mind that the evaluators are themselves social scientists. Non-utilisation of social science knowledge is not only a waste, but also the source of wrong expectations. By using and testing, the public will also become scientifically enlightened and informed, while through application, the social sciences will renew and revitalise themselves. Awareness of the power of a theory to predict might assist in the process of 'testing' a theory of social science. The problems of using prediction as a validating test are, nevertheless, considerable, even in the natural sciences. How could it be applied, for example, to the science of cosmology, with a time scale of millions of years hence? Indeed, what of the inability of Darwinian theory to predict even in general terms the future course of evolution? Michael Scriven, in his essay, 'Explanation and prediction in evolutionary theory'[62] comments that

Darwin demonstrated that a science can give a satisfactory explanation of the past even when prediction of the future is impossible.

(IX) Bringing new and substantiated knowledge found in natural sciences to the social sciences. It is necessary to establish systematic, two-way, academic channels to provide a constant flow of new knowledge between the social sciences arid the natural sciences. This flow of knowledge will strengthen the scientific foundation for the former and create new areas of research for both. We may quote a few examples: The Human Genome Project has created a wealth of possibilities for social research, a well as cooperative cross-disciplinary inquiries; for instance a systematic, coordinated undertaking to study the ethical, legal, social and educational issues which may arise.

In biotechnology research it is envisaged that revolutionary advancement will generate vital new products that would undoubtedly change the modes of production and consumption as well as the economy and civilisation as a whole in the twenty-first century. For instance, the conversion of methane into carbon dioxide, sugar and protein would certainly affect agriculture and food supply, demand and distribution.

67

In computer science, it is predicted that in the foreseeable future, satellite computers will guide the operation of agriculture and forestry equipment. These computers can sense precisely how much nutrients and water individual plants and vegetables need for optimal outputs and when to command the equipment to function. Satellite computers can be used extensively to conduct accurate and speedy research in the social sciences and related fields, such as geology, geography, history, politics, and population studies, just to name a few.

Another rapidly advancing field is cosmological research. By 2003, it will enable scientists to answer the question where mass comes from. And in 2008, a Mars lander will return to Earth with soil samples. If a strand of DNA is found there, then the most challenging question since the Darwinian evolution will have arisen: who is a human being? What is man's position in the Universe? As a result of new discoveries in natural sciences, social scientists will have to review their inquiries in order to reinterpret their significance.

An early attempt to bring psychological studies and neurological research together was found in the efforts of Donald O. Hebb some forty-five years ago.[63] Cross-fertilisation of knowledge would allow social scientists to gain not only new insights but also new expertise in the scientific adventure.

It is tempting to consider specifically not only 'the idea of science' but the whole problem of what is acceptable as *'scientific explanation'*. Philosopher of science, Carl Hempel addresses it in his central thesis,[64] of which an outline is attempted below, and which can be seen to have relevance to the 'new approach' to social science suggested in this study. It hinges on the nature of the two parts of 'scientific explanation': a statement of the event to be explained (the *explanandum)* and the statement which constitutes the explanation itself (the *explanans)*. The *explanans* has to be a general law which has universal application to the class of events of which the *explanandum* is an example. It must be possible to deduce, in logical fashion, the *explanandum* from the *explanans* which must be, in every sense, true. Following a statement of antecedent conditions, the entire content of the *explanandum* must be empirical, the *explanandum* seen as logically required by the *explanans*. With his advocacy of the use of teleological analysis in the study of purposive behaviour, an area of particular significance in the social sciences, Hempel disagrees with the assertion that 'a causal type of explanation is inadequate in fields other than physics and chemistry'.

It could be to the advantage of learning theory if some universally accepted framework of adequacy of explanation were adopted, in relation to, say, Piaget's stages of intellectual development theory or Skinner's reinforcement hypotheses. Though, because of the stance taken on what exactly is the nature of social science, some of the literature quoted in this study does not see the need, the measures recommended above signify a re-direction of the development of the social sciences *in general* from superficiality to profundity, from triviality to comprehensiveness, from dispersive to cumulative, and from empirical to scientific inquiry. Progress would be slow in the beginning, but it is bound to accelerate, forming a strong and vital component, an ongoing enterprise in human civilisation.

69

Notes

1   Paul Kennedy. *Preparing for the Twenty-first Century.* New York: Random House, 1993. Citing historical references and current data, the author forecasts a depressing picture for the future. Enduring problems concerning population, migration, robotics and automation, environment and natural resources, and others. will persist and multiply, and therefore existing theories about and methods of dealing with them will lose whatever effectiveness they might have today. Kennedy is the author of another provocative book entitled *The Rise and Fall of the Great Powers: Economic Change and Military Conflict from 1500 to 2000.* New York: Random House, 1987.

2   Peter T. Manicas, in *A History and Philosophy of the Social Sciences* (Oxford and New York: Basil Blackwell, 1987), indicated that '(t)he social sciences, complete with the now familiar disciplinary divisions, emerge in a recognisably modern form no earlier than the end of the nineteenth century' (p.7) as a response of the academic community to the challenge of the era of industrialisation to produce scientific explanations of various social problems and changes (pp.3-6). In 'The Many Meanings of Research Utilization' (1979) published in *Public Administration Review* 39(5) (pp 426-431) Carol H. Weiss discusses a number of alternative models for social science research to impact public policy making.

3   Tom Brokaw's interview with Janet Reno, U.S. Attorney General, NBC News, 11 p.m., April 19, 1993.

4   The case of Schmidt v. DeBoer was reported in detail in the *Ann Arbor News* of Ann Arbor, Michigan, where the case was litigated, during the months of January through April, 1993.

5   John D. Barrow, *Pi in the Sky.* Oxford and New York: Oxford University Press, 1992, pp. 164-65. See also: Terrence E. Cook (1994) *Criteria of Social Scientific Knowledge: Interpretation, Prediction, Praxis.* Lanham MD: Rowan and Littlefield; also Steven C. Ward (1996) *Reconfiguring Truth: Postmodernism, Science Studies and the Search for a New Model of Knowledge.* Lanham MD: Rowan and Littlefield Publishers.

6   Carl F. Kaestle, 'The Awful Reputation of Education Research', *Educational Researcher,* 22:1 (January-February 1993), pp.23-31. In a letter of Summer 1995 to Cho-Yee To, legal scholar L.B. Curzon wrote: 'I think that the mediocrity of much educational research reflects a failure to pose problems correctly, a reliance upon inadequate data, and a general ignorance of scientific method. In his article (June 1990) on 'My Conception of Economic Science', Professor Maurice Allais cites his 1988 Nobel lecture to stress that 'the prerequisite of any science is the existence of regularities which can be analysed and forecast...When neither the hypotheses nor the implications of a theory can be confronted with the real world, that theory is devoid of any scientific interest.. Any theory whatever, if it is not verified by empirical evidence, has no value and should be rejected...' Had these criteria been observed we might have been spared much of the ephemeral trivia masquerading as 'educational research'. J.W. Getzels (1978) in 'Paradigm and Practice: On the Impact of Basic Research in Education' in *Knowledge for Policy: Improving Education through Research,* Don S. Anderson and Bruce J. Biddle (1991) eds, London. New York: The Falmer Press, provides examples of basic research impact and argues the centrality of theory.

72

7   In regard to education, see, for example, Hubert M. Blalock Jr.'s 'Dilemmas in Social Research', Chester E. Finn Jr.'s 'What Ails Education Research', and Henry M. Levin's 'Why Isn't Educational Research More Useful' all of which can be found in Don S. Anderson and Bruce J. Biddle's *Knowledge For Policy: Improving Education through Research.* London. New York: The Falmer Press. 1991. A refutation is given by Richard J. Savelson and David C. Berliner (1991) in the Anderson and Biddle volume: 'Erosion of the Education Research Structure: A Reply to Finn'. John Ziman in *Reliable Knowledge: An Exploration* of *the Grounds for Belief in Science* Cambridge and New York: Cambridge University Press, 1991 (1978), (pp. 158-186) points out a number of limitations to which the social sciences are particularly susceptible. These limitations include a lack of sharply defined formal categories and a satisfactory mechanism for discovering significant categories, lack of a formal 'algebra' for specifying possible relations and patterns discovered among the categories, the simplicity of the experiments and observations and subsequent information derived from them, and reliance upon highly speculative hidden

variables. In summing up, Ziman writes, 'it might be said that the behavioural sciences are cluttered with innumerable half-articulated models.. that have never been subjected to critical validation. Standards of theory construction and confirmation have seldom been sufficiently high to distinguish clearly between what is well established, what is essentially conjectural, and what has been thoroughly disconfirmed' (p. 171). Henry H. Bauer in *Scientific Literacy and the Myth of the Scientific Method.* Urbana and Chicago: University of Illinois Press, 1992, (pp. 128-140) also states that the social sciences are not science because they admit to no 'body of agreed-upon and to-be-relied-upon knowledge' (p.131), 'possess no (single) governing paradigm' generating unresolvable disagreement among 'factions' (p.133), and rely more on methodological soundness than on 'reality therapy' (pp. 134-138), all of which contribute to a lack of consensus.

8   Here John Ziman echoes Thomas Kuhn's interpretation of paradigms as fundamental to science as a social process. See Ziman, *Reliable Knowledge An Exploration of the Grounds for Belief in Science.* Cambridge and New York: Cambridge University Press, 1991 (1978). p.90. Also, see Thomas S. Kuhn, *The Structure of Scientific Revolutions.* Chicago: The University of Chicago Press, 1970, p. 109. Henry H. Bauer offers a similar observation, saying that 'social science cannot bring itself to recognise that what truly does characterise science is consensus induced by reality therapy and attested by an established paradigm.' See Bauer, *Scientific Literacy and the Myth of the Scientific Method.* Urbana and Chicago: University of Illinois Press, 1992, p.137. It has been suggested that Kuhn replaced the term 'paradigm' with 'disciplinary matrices' and 'exemplars'; essentially, however, the concept of 'paradigm' is valuable. See also: Barry Barnes (1982) *T.S. Kuhn and Social Science.* Boston: Houghton Mifflin Company.

9   This is Karl Popper's criterion. See Popper, *Conjectures and Refutations.* New York: Harper and Row. 1962. Falsifiability has generated many variants since Popper first proposed it. Verifiability, testability, refutability, etc., are alternative demarcation criteria that have the common notion of confronting a theory with empirical fact. See also: Karl Popper's (1963) 'Science: Conjecture and Refutations' in Janet A. Kourany (1987) ed. *Scientific Knowledge.* Belmont CA: Wadsworth Inc. Imre

73

Lakatos (1970) looks at falsification in his 'Falsification and the Methodology of Scientific Research Programmes' published in the Kourany (1987) volume above.

10 Ernest Gellner, 'The Scientific Status of the Social Sciences,' in his *Relativism and the Social Sciences.* Cambridge and New York: Cambridge University Press, 1985, p. 115.

11 For reference see three recent publications: Peter T. Manicas' *A History and Philosophy of the Social Sciences.* Oxford and New York: Basil Blackwell, Ltd. 1987, Dorothy Ross' *The Origins of American Social Science.* Cambridge and New York: Cambridge University Press, 1991, and M. Mitchell Waldrop's *Complexity:The Emerging Science at the Edge of Order and Chaos.* New York: Simon and Schuster.

12 Paul Diesing, (1991) *How Does Social Science Work? Reflections on Practice.* Pittsburgh: University of Pittsburgh Press. In his book, Diesing describes a hierarchical structure of communities with social science itself as the largest community. Within social science there are such distinct disciplines as sociology and economics all claiming their own separate domains. The third level works within or across disciplines and is characterised by adherence to a particular philosophical or dogmatic position on why, how, and what to research. The smallest communities are 'schools of thought' or research programmes characterised by a more specific philosophical position and topic of interest and composed of individuals 'who frequently communicate and build on each other's work' (p. 339). Diesing gives three causes for the flourishing of research programmes, the first of which is the founding of a research programme based on a strong social concern for or interest in current developments in the world or social science community. These new research programmes often result from the appearance of a new book expressing a new theory or idea, such as Keynes' *The General Theory of Employment, Interest, and Money* or Skinner's *The Behavior of Organisms.* The other two causes concern funding agencies, governments, and corporations, the primary sponsors of social science research and supporting only research that is important to them. See also: Thomas D. Cook (1985) 'Postpositivist Criticism, Reforms Associations, and Uncertainties about Social Research' in Don S. Anderson and Bruce J. Biddle (1991) eds, *Knowledge for Policy: Improving Education through Research.* London. New York: The Falmer

Press for his views on authority in social sciences. Ahmed Gurnah and Alan Scott (1992) *The Uncertain Science: Criticism of Sociological Formalism.* London and New York: Routledge who see sociology as but a handmaiden of philosophy address its weaknesses given in the explanations above, especially the first. Paul Thagard (1992) *Conceptual Revolution.* Princeton NJ: Princeton University Press.

13 Using an identical method of analysis (see Appendix), doctoral students Mary Jo May, Trevor Leutscher, and Helen Marks, all of the University of Michigan, Ann Arbor, completed three parallel studies on theory formation of Piaget, Skinner, and Kohlberg, respectively, under the direction of Cho-Yee To, Professor of Education. These studies used as many primary sources as available and were supplemented by secondary references. See Cho-Yee To, Trevor J. Leutscher, Mary Jo May, and Helen M. Marks' *Formation of a Theory:Piaget, Skinner, and Kolhberg (Draft Research Report).* The University of Michigan, Ann Arbor, Philosophy of Education Seminar, Fall 1990. Unpublished manuscript.

14 See Mary Jo May's 'Piaget' (pp.7-8 and 13-14) in Cho-Yee To, Trevor I. Leutscher, Mary Jo May, and Helen M. Marks' *Formation of a Theory: Piaget, Skinner, and Kolhberg (Draft Research Report).* The University of Michigan, Ann Arbor, Philosophy of Education Seminar, Fall 1990. Unpublished manuscript. In her study, May notes that some scholars regarded Piaget's expression of constructivist, structuralist, or interactionist positions as his most important contributions, others consider the concept of equilibration or the conceptualisation of the mind's restructuring through assimilation, then accommodation, and finally adaptation to facts of reality as his most important contributions.

15 See R. Evans' *Jean Piaget: The Man and His Ideas* (E. Duckworth, Translator). New York: E.P. Dutton, 1973.

16 See May's 'Piaget,' p.32 and p.35.

17 Sohan Modgil and Celia Modgil (1987) eds, *B.F. Skinner: consensus and controversy.* London and New York: The Falmer Press, 1987. p.11

18 B.F. Skinner 'Whatever Happened to Psychology as the Science of Behavior', *American Psychologist,* 1987 42 (8), pp.780-786.

19 See, for example, Robert W. Proctor and Daniel J. Weeks' *The Goal of B.F. Skinner and Behavior Analysis.* New York:

75

Springer-Verlag, 1990 or Norman Guttman's 'On Skinner and Hull: A Reminiscence and Projection', *American Psychologist,* 1977 32 (5)

20 Helen M. Marks' 'Kohlberg', In Cho-Yee To, Trevor J. Leutscher, Mary Jo May, and Helen M. Marks', *Formation of a Theory: Piaget, Skinner, and Kohlberg (Draft Research Report).* The University of Michigan, Ann Arbor, Philosophy of Education Seminar, Fall 1990, p.6. Unpublished manuscript.

21 Ibid., p.16.

22 Ibid., p.18. From Lawrence Kohlberg's *Essays in Moral Development Vol* IL *The Psychology of Moral Development.* San Francisco: Harper and Row. 1984.

23 See Power, F.C., A. Higgins, and L. Kohlberg (1989) *Lawrence Kohlberg Approach to Moral Education.* New York: Columbia University Press; Reimer, J., D.P. Paolitto, and R.H. Hersh (1983). *Promoting Moral Growth From Piaget to Kohlberg.* 2nd Edition. New York: Longmans; and Modgil, S. and C. Modgil (1986), *Lawrence Kohlberg: Consensus and Controversy.* Philadelphia: Falmer Press.

24 Stephen J. Gould (1996) in *The Mismeasure of Man.* Harmondsworth: The Penguin Press, examines the problem and its consequences

25 See Paul Diesing (1991) *How Does Social Science Work? Reflections on Practice.* Pittsburgh: University of Pittsburgh Press (pp 112-124, 348-349) and C.Owen Paepke (1993) *The Evolution of Progress: The End of Economic Growth and the Beginning of Human Transformation.* New York: Random House, Inc.

26 Two works of Schön's have been particularly influential. See: David Schön (1983) *The Reflective Practitioner.* London: Temple Smith and (1987) *Educating the Reflective Practitioner.* San Francisco: Jossey Bass. In England Paul Hirst has been identified with attempts to separate 'theory' from 'practice' in teacher education. See Paul Hirst (1990) 'The theory-practice relationship in teacher training' in: Martin Booth, John Furlong and Margaret Wilkin, eds, *Partnership in Initial Teacher Training.* London: Cassell and the same (1995) 'Education, knowledge and practice' in Robin Barrow and Patricia White, eds, *Beyond Liberal Education.* London and New York: Routledge.

27 These are the dissertation proposals selected and submitted with strong recommendations by social science departments to the graduate school in the academic years 1987-88, 88-89, and 89-90. About 40% of these proposals succeeded in obtaining research grants. Disciplines represented by these proposals include: Anthropology; Business Administration; Economics; Education; History; Information and Library Science; Health Services, Organisation and Policy; Landscape Architecture; Natural Resources; Nursing; Planning, and Urban Technology and Environmental Planning. The 'Rackham Theory Used Table' was compiled by the research team consisting of Mary Jo May, Trevor J. Leutscher and Helen Marks under the supervision of Professor Cho-Yee To. See Note 14 above.

28 A compilation reveals that only four of the seventeen researchers monitored as using multiple theories justified their use.

29 An interesting discussion on personality influences is found in Chapter 10 of Paul Diesing's *How Does Social Science Work? Reflections on Practice,* quoted before. Chapter 8 of the book examines the politics of social research claims that the emphasis in the research and publication agendas is not arbitrary but 'reflects the successive concerns of the funding agencies' (p.239). In reviewing the literature on cognitive processes in social science (Chapter 9) Diesing depicts a characteristic of social science where social science researchers appear more susceptible to retaining expectations (theories) based on background knowledge despite the discovery of contrary evidence (pp.245-254 and pp.269-270). That is, social theories possess a characteristic of social perpetuity because disciples of a theory or approach strive to rationalise or ignore contradictory evidence rather than discard their intuitive beliefs. John Coates' justification of 'common sense' for relaxing the rules of language and methods of procedure brings the concept of 'empathy with the subject matter' into the discussion of purposeful science. Coates (1996): *The Claims of Common Sense: Moore, Wittgenstein, Keynes and the Social Sciences.* Cambridge: Cambridge University Press.

30 The term 'methodology' is incorrectly used by a good number of researchers in both the natural and social sciences – but especially the latter. Nowadays it means research methods and procedures employed in some complicated and sophisticated

77

fashion. The original, and still philosophical, meaning of the term is the study of method. Fritz Machlup in his *Methodology of Economics and Other Social Sciences.* New York: Academic Press, 1978 states: 'Although methodology is about methods, it is not a method, nor a set of methods, nor a description of methods... while we use a method, we never 'use' methodology; and while we may describe a method, we cannot 'describe' methodology'.

31 Sylvain Bromberger's (1992) *On What We Know We* Don't *Know: Explanation, Theory, Linguistics, and How Questions Shape Them.* Chicago: University of Chicago Press demon strates the way questions can be put in such a way that they answer themselves.

32 Works on this topic that have been reviewed include those by Henry Bauer, Paul Diesing, Ernest Gellner, Thomas Kuhn, Fritz Machlup, Ernest Nagel, Karl Popper, John Ziman, among others. Some of their works have been collected in Janet A. Kourany's *Scientific Knowledge.* Belmont CA: Wadsworth, Inc. See bibliography. See also: *Natural Sciences and the Social Sciences: Some Critical and Historical perspectives.* Boston MA: Kluwer Academic 1994.

33 Ernest Gellner (1985) *Relativism and the Social Sciences.* Cambridge and New York: Cambridge University Press (p.12).

34 Even within one of the systems, between disciplines within the system (e.g. physics and chemistry), or between sub-disciplines of one of these disciplines (e.g. solid state physics and particle physics), the specific criteria for what constitutes scientific evidence and accuracy may differ fundamentally.

35 A. Charles Catania and Stevan Hamad (1988) eds, The *Selection of Behaviour: The Operant Behaviourism of B F Skinner, Comments and Consequences.* Cambridge: Cambridge University Press.

36 Dynamic invariances refer to the properties that change but can be specified formally as functions, e.g. laws of conservation.

37 Consider the case of the purported discovery and demonstration of cold fusion. 'When it was reported that an experiment generating a fusion reaction without producing high temperatures and the need for containment had been conducted, other scientists were understandably sceptical. As a consequence these independent investigators attempted to replicate the pro-

cedures and results. The failure to obtain the same effects forced rejection of the initially reported results.

38   For example, Coulomb's 'law' states that the electrostatic attraction or repulsion between electrically charged bodies is directly proportional to the product of the electric charges on each body, and inversely proportional to the square of the distance between the bodies. Coulomb's law describes the attraction and repulsion property of charged bodies. Scientists do not attempt to explain this fundamental observation about the physical world: they are not theologians. However, Coulomb's law can help to explain other phenomena. These kinds of fundamental laws describe patterns in nature; they thus have predictive power.

39   The empirical base of Freudian theory is questionable, as reported by Frank J. Solloway, a professor of science history at the Massachussets Institute of Technology, at the 1990 annual conference of the American Association for the Advancement of Science. See also 'Freudian Slippery? Scientists Dispute The Research Basis of His Theories' by Paul Recer of the Associated Press in The Ann Arbor News, February 18, 1991, pp.A1 and A11, and Elizabeth Stone, 'Off the Couch', *New York Times Magazine*, December 6, 1992, pp 49-81.

40   See B.F. Skinner's 'Whatever Happened to Psychology as the Science of Behavior?' *American Psychologist,* 1987, 42 (8), pp.780-786.

41   See Harald Clahsen (1992) 'Learnability Theory and the Problem of Development in Language Acquisition' In: J.Weissenborn, H. Goodluck and T.Roepers, eds, *Theoretical Issues in Language Acquisition*. Hillsdale NJ. Hove and London: Lawrence Erlbaum.

42   In Newtonian mechanics one could take the sum or difference of any two velocities, i.e. when an observer is moving the velocity of an object would appear to be moving at its velocity plus or minus the velocity of the observer. According to Einstein, the velocity of light is the same for all observers, whether stationary or moving. Hence the speed of light becomes a reference according to which observations in frames of reference must be related. See also: Gilles Cohen-Tannoudji (1993, 1991) *Universal Constants in Physics.* New York: McGraw-Hill., Inc.

43   In his *Making Science: Between Nature and Society.* Cambridge MA: Harvard University Press (1992) Stephen Cole does not

make a distinction between the validity of the social and natural sciences, while Harold Kincaid (1996) in his stimulating *Philosophical Foundations of the Social Sciences: Analysing Controversies in Social Research.* (Cambridge: Cambridge University Press) argues that social science can be a 'good' science.

44 Ernest Gellner, *Relativism and the Social Sciences.* Cambridge and New York: Cambridge University Press, 1985, pp.83-85.

45 The chapters by James Flynn 'Race and IQ: Jensen's Case Refuted' and Arthur Jensen's 'Differential Psychology: Towards Consensus' in the volume *Arthur Jensen Consensus and Controversy* edited by Sohan Modgil and Celia Modgil, New York. London: The Falmer Press, 1987 give good arguments for the opposing views on the IQ tests. See also: Richard J. Herrnstein and Charles Murray, *The Bell Curve: Intelligence and Class Structure in American Life.* New York: Free Press, 1994. More details of the racist implications can be found in J. Philippe Rushton, *Race Evolution and Behaviour. A Life History Perspective.* New Brunswick, NJ: Transaction, 1994.

46 A cover statement from Robert Shapiro's *The Human Blueprint: The Race to unlock the Secrets of Our Genetic Code.* New York: Bantam Books, 1992 (1991).

47 An internet search on the Human Genome Project in January 1999 turned up many pages of information. A brief introduction is as follows: Begun in 1990, the Human Genome Project is a 15-year effort coordinated by the US Department of Energy and the National Institute of Health to (1) identify all the estimated 80.000 genes in human DNA, and (2) determine the sequences of the 3 billion chemical bases that make up human DNA, store this information in databases, and develop tools for a data analysis. To help achieve these goals, researchers are also studying the genetic makeup of several non-human organisms. These include the common human gut bacterium *Escherichia coli,* the fruit fly, and the laboratory mouse. A unique aspect of the US Human Genome Project is that it is the first large scientific undertaking to address the ethical, legal, and social issues (ELSI) that may arise from the project. (Ref.: URL: www.ornl.gov/hgmis).

48 The quotation comes from *A Source Book in Chinese Philosophy,* translated and compiled by Wing-Tsit Chan (Princeton NJ: Princeton University Press, 1969, page: 40).

49 For instance, although references from both the natural sciences and the social sciences express similar characteristics for 'theory,' the definitions differ in regard to what kinds of entities a theory should explain. Indeed, one social science definition, in addition to prediction, states that theory can 'prescribe conduct,' which would not be regarded as legitimate in the natural sciences. See also: Robert K. Barnhart's (1986) *The American Heritage Dictionary of Science.* Boston MA: Houghton Mifflin Company.

50 As the division between natural science and social science begins to blur, it would also be necessary to include natural scientists among the members of this editorial board so as to not isolate the social sciences from the broader scientific community. This editorial board should be comprised of scholars in all fields of science, supported by the professional organisations to which they belong. It certainly should not be a government project.

51 This is the ten-point analysis model used for the studies of Piaget, Skinner, and Kohlberg. See Appendix.

52 Academic conferences in the social sciences are gatherings of interest groups or collections of unrelated, eclectic presentations. If the idea of 'theory challenge' recommended in this paper is adopted, the routine convention could become a vital event for acknowledging research advancement (other than presentation) for the social sciences. See also: C.Wade Savage (1990) *Scientific Theories: Minnesota Studies in the Philosophy of Science.* V. XIV. Minneapolis: University of Minnesota Press.

53 See: S.Pit Corder (1991) 'A Role for the Mother Tongue' in: S.M. Gass and L. Selinker, eds, *Language Transfer in Language Learning.* Amsterdam. Philadelphia: John Benjamins Publishing Company; also: Robert Politzer (1974) 'Developmental sentence scoring as a method' in: *Modern Language Journal* 58 and: Helmut Zobl (1984) 'Cross-generalisations and the Contrastive Dimension of the Interlanguage Hypothesis' in: Alan Davies, Clive Criper and A.P.R. Howatt, eds, *Interlanguage.* Edinburgh: Edinburgh University Press.

54 See, for example, Piaget's *Genetic Epistemology* (E. Duckworth, Translator), New York: Columbia, 1977. The *Development of Thought: Equilibration of Cognitive Structures* (A. Rosin, Translator), New York: Viking Press, 1977 (1975), and

Adaptation and Intelligence: Organic Selection and Phenocopy (S. Eames, Translator), Chicago: University of Chicago Press, 1980 (1974).

55 See, for instance, Skinner's 'The Science of Learning and the Art of Teaching', *Harvard Education Review, 24,* 1954, pp.86-97; 'Why We Need Teaching Machines', *Harvard Education Review,* 31, 1961, pp.377-398; 'Reflections on a Decade of Teaching Machines', *Teachers College Record,* 65, 1963, pp. 168-177; 'Contingency Management in the Classroom', *Education, 90,*1969, pp.93-100; *The Technology of Teaching,* New York: Appleton-Century-Croft, 1968, and 'Programmed Instruction Revisited', *Phi Delta Kappan, 68(2),* October 1986, pp. 103-110.

56 See, for example, Kohlberg's *Essays in Moral Development: Vol. II. The Psychology of Moral Development.* San Francisco: Harper and Row, 1984 and *Child Psychology and Childhood Education: A Cognitive-developmental View.* New York: Longmans, 1987.

57 See also Barnhart's *The American Heritage Dictionary of Science* (1986) quoted above. John Coates' *The Claims of Common Sense: Moore, Wittgenstein, Keynes and the Social Sciences.* (Cambridge: Cambridge University Press, 1996) examines the 'vague' terminology used by the three social scientists discussed.

58 See also: *From Positivism to Interpretivism and Beyond: Tales of Transformation in Educational and Social Research (The Mind-Body Connection).* New York: Teachers College Press, 1997.

59 See: Steve Joshua Heims (1993) *Constructing a Social Science for Postwar America: the Cybernetics Group, 1946-1953.* Cambridge MA: The MIT Press.

60 Michael Scriven (1967) 'The contribution of philosophy of the social sciences to educational development' in: *Philosophy and Educational Development.* (H.D. Aiken, W. Kaufman and M. Scriven, eds, London: G.H. Harrap Ltd).

61 See: Paul Humphreys (1989) *The Chances of Explanation: Causal Explanation in the Social, Medical, and Physical Sciences.* Princeton NJ: Princeton University Press.

62 Michael Scriven (1959) 'Explanation and prediction in evolutionary theory' *Science,* no.130.

63 Peter M. Milner 'The Mind and Donald O. Hebb', *Scientific American*, 1993 Vol 274.1 pp. 124-129. Also: Patricia Smith Churchland (1986) *Neurophilosophy: Toward a Unified Science of the Mind-Brain.* Cambridge MA: The MIT Press.

64 Carl G. Hempel (1965) *Aspects of Scientific Explanation and Other Essays in the Philosophy of Science:* New York: The Free Press, (London: Collier-MacMillan Ltd.). Steven C. Ward (1996) *Reconfiguring Truth: Postmodernism, Science Studies, and the Search for a New Model of Knowledge.* Lanham MD: Rowan and Littlefield.

Bibliography

Anderson, Don S., and Bruce J. Biddle (1991) *Knowledge for Policy: Improving Education through Research.* London and New York: The Falmer Press

Barnes, Barry (1982) *T.S. Kuhn and Social Science.* New York: Columbia University Press

Barnhart, Robert K. (1986) *The American Heritage Dictionary of Science.* Boston MA: Houghton Mifflin Company

Barrow, John D. (1992) *Pi in the Sky: Counting, Thinking, and Being.* Oxford: Clarendon Press

Bauer, Henry H. (1992) S*cientific Literacy and the Myth of the Scientific Method.* Urbana and Chicago: University of Illinois Press

Blalock, Hubert M., Jr. (1991 (1984)) 'Dilemmas in Social Research' In: Don S. Anderson and Bruce J. Biddle *Knowledge for Policy: Improving Education through Research.* London and New York: The Falmer Press

Bromberger, Sylvain (1992) *On What We Know We Don't Know: Explanation, Theory, Linguistics, and How Questions Shape them.* Chicago: University of Chicago Press

Cartwright, Dorwin (1991 (1949)) 'Basic and Applied Social Psychology' In: Don S. Anderson and Bruce J. Biddle *Knowledge for Policy: Improving Education through Research.* London and New York: The Falmer Press

Catania, Charles, A. and Stevan Harnad, Eds (1988) *The Selection of Behaviour: The Operant Behaviourism of B.F. Skinner. Comments of Consequences.* Cambridge: Cambridge University Press

Churchland, Patricia Smith (1986) *Neurophilosophy: Toward a Unified* Science *of the Mind-Brain.* Cambridge MA: The MIT Press

Coates, John (1996) *The Claims of Common Sense: Moore, Wittgenstein, Keynes and the Social Sciences.* Cambridge: Cambridge University Press

Cohen, David K., and Michael S. Garet (1991 (1975)) 'Reforming Educational Policy with Applied Social Research' In: Don S. Anderson and Bruce J. Biddle *Knowledge for Policy: Improving Education through Research.* London and New York: The Falmer Press

Cohen-Tannoudji, Gilles (1993 (1991)) *Universal Constants in Physics.* New York: McGraw Hill

Cole, Stephen (1992) *Making Science: Between Nature and Society.* Cambridge MA: Harvard University Press

Constructive Criticism: The Human Sciences in the Age of Theory. (1995) Toronto: University of Toronto Press

Cook, Terrence E. (1994) *Criteria of Social Scientific Knowledge: Interpretation, Prediction, Praxis.* Lanham MD: Rowan and Little-field

Cook, Thomas D. (1991 (1985)) 'Postpositivist Criticism, Reforms Associations, and Uncertainties about Social Research' In: Don S. Anderson and Bruce J. Biddle *Knowledge for Policy: Improving Education through Research.* London and New York: The Falmer Press

Diesing, Paul (1991) *How Does Social Science Work: Reflections on Practice.* Pittsburgh: University of Pittsburgh Press

Duhem, Pierre (1991 (1906)) *The Aim and Structure of Physical Theory.* Princeton NJ: Princeton University Press

Evans, Robert (1973) *Jean Piaget: The Man and His Ideas.* (translated by E. Duckworth) New York: E.P. Dutton

Finn, Chester E., Jr (1991 (1988)) 'What Ails Education Research' In: Don S. Anderson and Bruce J. Biddle *Knowledge for Policy: Improving through Research.* London and New York: The Falmer Press

Fox, Robin (1997) *Conjectures and Confrontations: Science, Evolution, Social Concern.* New Brunswick NJ: Transaction

From Positivism to Interpretivism and Beyond: Tales of Transformation in Educational and Social Research (The Mind-Body Connection) (1997) New York: Teachers College Press

Gellner, Ernest (1985) *Relativism and the Social Sciences.* Cambridge and New York: Cambridge University Press

Getzels, J. W. (1991 (1978)) 'Paradigm and Practice: On the Impact of Basic Research in Education' In: Don S. Anderson and Bruce J.

Biddle, *Knowledge for Policy: Improving Education through Research*. London and New York: The Falmer Press

Gould, Stephen, J. (1996) *The Mismeasure of Man*. Harmondsworth: Penguin

Guba, Egon G., and Yvonna S. Lincoln (1991 (1989)) 'What is the Constructivist Paradigm?' In: Don S. Anderson and Bruce J. Biddle *Knowledge for Policy: Improving Education through Research*. London and New York: The Falmer Press

Gurnah, Ahmed, and Alan Scott (1992) *The Uncertain Science: Criticism of Sociological Formalism*. London and New York: Routledge

Guttman, Norman (1977) 'On Skinner and Hull: A Reminiscence and Projection' *American Psychologist* 32(5)

Halton, Eugene (1995) *Bereft of Reason: On the Decline of Social Thought* and *Prospects for its Renewal*. Chicago: University of Chicago Press

Heims, Steve Joshua (1993) *Constructing a Social Science for Post-war America: the Cybernetics Group, 1946-1953*. Cambridge MA: The MIT Press

Hempel, Carl G. (1965) *Aspects of Scientific Explanation and Other Essays in the Philosophy of Science*. New York: The Free Press

Hernstein, Richard J. and Charles Murray (1994) *The Bell Curve: Intelligence and Class Structure in American Life*. New York: The Free Press

Hirst, Paul (1990) 'The theory-practice relationship in teacher training' In: Martin Booth, John Furlong and Margaret Wilkin, Eds, *Partnership in Initial Teacher Training*. London: Cassell

Hirst, Paul (1995) 'Education knowledge and practice' In: Robin Barrow and Patricia White, Eds, *Beyond Liberal Education*. London and Sydney: Routledge

Humphreys, Paul (1989) *The Chances of Explanation: Causal Explanation in the Social, Medical, and Physical Sciences*. Princeton NJ: Princeton University Press

Kaestle, Carl, F. (1993) 'The Awful Reputation of Education Research' *Educational Research*. 22.1

Kennedy, Paul (1987) *The Rise and Fall of the Great Powers: Economic Change and Military Conflict from 1500 to 2000*. New York: Random House

87

Kennedy, Paul (1993) *Preparing for the Twenty-first Century.* New York: Random House

Kerlinger, Fred N. (1991 (1979)) 'Science and Behavioral Research' In: Don S. Anderson and Bruce J. Biddle *Knowledge for Policy: Improving Education through Research.* London and New York: The Falmer Press

Keynes, John M. for original writings see notes 12 and 56

Kincaid, Harold (1996) *Philosophical Foundations of the Social Sciences: Analysing Controversies in Social Research.* Cambridge: Cambridge University Press

Kohlberg, Lawrence for original writings see notes 22 and 55

Kourany, Janet A. (1987) *Scientific Knowledge.* Belmont CA: Wadsworth

Kuhn, Thomas (1970 (1962)) *The Structure of Scientific Revolutions* (second edition, enlarged), Chicago: University of Chicago Press

Kuhn, Thomas (1987 (1963)) 'The Function of Dogma in Scientific Research' In: Kourany, Janet A., Ed. *Scientific Knowledge.* Belmont CA: Wadsworth

Kuhn, Thomas (1987 (1970)) 'The Nature and Necessity of Scientific Revolutions' In: Kourany, Janet A., Ed. *Scientific Knowledge.* Belmont CA: Wadsworth

Kuhn, Thomas (1987 (1977)) 'Objectivity, Value Judgement, and Theory Choice' In: Kourany, Janet A., Ed. *Scientific Knowledge.* Belmont CA: Wadsworth

Lakatos, Imre (1987 (1970)) 'Falsification and the Methodology of Scientific Research Programmes' In: Kourany, Janet A., Ed. *Scientific Knowledge.* Belmont CA: Wadsworth

Laudan, Larry (1987 (1984)) 'Dissecting the Holist Picture of Scientific Change' In: Kourany, Janet A., Ed. *Scientific Knowledge.* Belmont CA: Wadsworth

Levin, Henry M. (1991 (1978)) 'Why Isn't Educational Research More Useful?' In: Don S. Anderson and Bruce J. Biddle *Knowledge for Policy: Improving Education through Research.* London and New York: The Falmer Press

Machlup, Fritz (1987) *Methodology of Economics and Other Social Sciences.* New York: Academic Press

Manicas, Peter T. (1987) *A History and Philosophy of the Social Sciences.* Oxford and New York: Basil Blackwell

McIntyre, Lee C. (1996) *Laws and Explanation in the Social Sciences: Defending a Science of Human Behavior.* Boulder CO: Westview Press

Milner, Peter M. (1993) 'The Mind and Donald O. Hebb' *Scientific American* 56.1

Modgil, Sohan and Celia, Modgil, Eds (1987) *B.F. Skinner: Consensus and Controversy.* London and New York: The Falmer Press

Modgil, Sohan and Celia, Modgil Eds (1987) *Arthur Jensen: Consensus and Controversy.* New York and London: The Falmer Press

Nagel, Ernest (1987 (1979)) *The Structure of Science: Problems in the Logic of Scientific Explanation.* (second edition) Indianapolis IN: Hackett

Natural Sciences and the Social Sciences: Some Critical and Historical Perspectives. (1994) Boston MA: Kluwer

Oppenheim, Paul and Hilary Putnam (1987 (1958)) 'Unity of Science as a Working Hypothesis' In: Kourany, Janet A., Ed. *Scientific Knowledge.* Belmont CA: Wadsworth

Paepke, C. Owen (1993) *The Evolution of Progress: The End of Economic Growth and the Beginning of Human Transformation.* New York: Random House

Piaget, Jean: for original works in translation see note 53.

Popper, Karl (1962) *Conjecture and Refutations.* New York: Harper and Row

Popper, Karl (1987 (1963)) 'Science: Conjecture and Refutations' In: Kourany, Janet A. Ed. *Scientific Knowledge.* Belmont CA: Wadsworth

Popper, Karl (1987 (1975)) 'The Rationality of Scientific Revolutions' In: Kourany, Janet A., Ed. *Scientific Knowledge.* Belmont CA: Wadsworth, Inc.

Proctor, Robert W. and Daniel J. Weeks (1990) *The Goal of B.F. Skinner and Behavior Analysis.* Berlin and New York: Springer-Verlag

Ross, Dorothy (1991) *The Origins of American Social Science.* Cambridge and New York: Cambridge University Press

Rushton, J. Philippe (1994) *Race Evolution and Behavior. A Life History Perspective.* New Brunswick NJ: Transaction

89

Samuelson, Paul A., and William Nordhaus (1985) *Economics*. (12th Edition) New York: McGraw Hill

Savage, C. Wade (1990) *Scientific Theories: Minnesota Studies in the Philosophy of Science. Vol. XIV.* Minneapolis: University of Minnesota Press

Schön, David (1983) *The Reflective Practitioner: How professionals think in action.* London: Temple Smith

Schön, David (1987) *Educating the Reflective Practitioner.* San Francisco: Jossey-Bass

Scriven, Michael (1959) 'Explanation and prediction in evolutionary theory' *Science.* no.130

Scriven, Michael (1967) 'The contribution of philosophy of the social sciences to educational development' In: H.D. Aiken, W. Kaufman and M. Scriven, Eds, *Philosophy and Educational Development.* London: G.H. Harrap

Searle, John R. (1992) *The Rediscovery of the Mind.* Cambridge: MA, The MIT Press

Shapiro, Robert (1992 (1991)) *The Human Blueprint: The Race to Unlock the Secret of our Genetic Code.* New York: Bantam Doubleday Dell

Shavelson, Richard J., and David C. Berliner (1991 (1988)) 'Erosion of the Education Research Infrastructure: A Reply to Finn' In: Don S. Anderson and Bruce J. Biddle, *Knowledge for Policy: Improving Education through Research.* London and New York: The Falmer Press

Skinner, Burrhus, F. for original works see notes 39 and 54: also 18

Thagard, Paul (1992) *Conceptual Revolution.* Princeton NJ: Princeton University Press

To, Cho-Yee, Trevor J. Leutscher, Mary Jo May and Helen Marks (1991) – Formation of a Theory: Piaget, Skinner and Kohlberg (Draft Research Report). (Ann Arbor): The University of Michigan, Ann Arbor, Philosophy of Education Seminar Fall 1990. Unpublished Manuscript.

Von Eckardt, Barbara (1993) *What is Cognitive Science?* Cambridge MA: The MIT Press

Waldrop, M. Mitchell (1992) *Complexity: The Emerging Science at the Edge of Order and Chaos.* New York: Simon and Schuster

Ward, Steven C. (1996) *Reconfiguring Truth: Postmodernism. Science Studies, and the Search for a New Model of Knowledge.* Lanham MD: Rowan and Littlefield

Weiss, Carol H. (1991 (1979)) 'The Many Meanings of Research Utilisation' In: Don S. Anderson and Bruce J. Biddle, *Knowledge for Policy: Improving Education through Research.* London and New York: The Falmer Press

Ziman, John (1991 (1978)) *Reliable Knowledge: An Exploration of the Grounds for Belief in Science.* (Canto Edition) Cambridge and New York: Cambridge University Press

Appendix

A Research Instrument for Analysing Social Science Theorists, their Theories and Influences

This research instrument was used by the author's graduate students at the University of Michigan in their reports on the evolution of the three social science theory constructions dealt with in detail in the book:

Trevor J. Leutscher (Skinner)
Mary Jo May (Piaget)
Helen M. Marks (Kohlberg)

Formation of a Theory: Piaget, Skinner, and Kohlberg
The Theorist and the Theory –
Analysis and Assessment
Data Review Instrument

1.   Describe the theorist's biographical and
     intellectual background:

    1.1   Give the theorist's full-name, birthplace,
      dates of birth and death, nationality and
      ethnicity.

        1.1.1.   Provide biographical information
         (parents' educational levels,
         occupations, siblings' ages,
         social/economic status).

        1.1.2.   What influenced the theorist in his
         early life?

    1.2.   Describe the theorist's primary/secondary
      education – (geographical region, school
      type):

        1.2.1.   List the theorist's colleges and
         qualifications obtained (where,
         majors/minors, degrees/awards).

        1.2.2.   What were the theorist's early
         occupations (if any)?

        1.2.3.   Describe the theorist's graduate
         studies – university, field of
         research, advisors, the theorist's
         dissertation.

        1.2.4.   What positions did the theorist hold
         early in his career?

       1.2.5.   What other fields interested the theorist?

2.   Survey some of the theorist's works:

    2.1.   Name the theorist's major works: books, journal articles, other (reviews, etc.).

    2.2.   Provide a comprehensive bibliography of the theorist.

    2.3.   Describe the theorist's scholarly productivity.

       2.3.1.   Identify the theorist's early writing.

       2.3.2.   Identify the theorist's most creative, productive stage.

       2.3.3.   What works were written later in life?

3.   Survey works written about the theorist:

    3.1.   Identify the major works about the theorist and his theory/theories:

       3.1.1.   Books

       3.1.2.   Journal articles

       3.1.3.   Other materials

    3.2.   What are the major contributions of the theorist's theory/theories?

    3.3.   Identify the major criticisms of the theorist's theory/theories and their nature.

    3.4.   How did the theorist respond to these criticisms?

4. How influential were the theorist's major theories during the theorist's lifetime, and how influential are they now?

4.1. How influential was the theorist at the height of his career?

4.1.1. What was the theorist's influence in learned associations and societies concerned with the field of study (any positions held by the theorist)?

4.1.2. What new programs about the theory/theories were started at universities or research institutions?

4.1.3. What research/dissertations were done on the theorist's theory/theories by others?

4.1.4. Were versions of the ideas discussed in popular journals?

4.2. How did political, geographical factors affect the influence of the theory/theories?

4.2.1. What did the theorist's own countrymen think of the theory/theories?

4.2.2. How did those outside the theorist's own country regard the theory/theories?

4.2.3. Were the domestic and international judgments similar, identical, or different?

4.3. Was/were the theorist's theory/theories controversial? In what ways?

    4.4. Can one find non-rational, emotional basis for the popularity of the theory/theories?

    4.5. What is the theorist's influence on his field/fields now?

5. How did the theorist develop his theory/theories?

    5.1. What were the theorist's major objectives?

    5.2. What was the cultural/social setting in which the theorist developed his theory/theories?

        5.2.1. Describe the tradition in which the theorist worked.

        5.2.2. What were the primary and secondary influences upon the theorist's work?

        5.2.3. What are the major theory/theories the theorist claims to refute?

    5.3. What was the theorist's rationale?

        5.3.1. What was the theorist's subject matter and substantive interest?

        5.3.2. Describe the types of theory/theories: taxonomic, axiomatic, discursive.

        5.3.3. What major metaphors were used by the theorist?

    5.4. What are the theorist's own views of his limitations?

5.5. Was/were the theory/theories revised? If so, how?

6. Describe and characterize the intellectual environment in which the theorist developed his theory/theories.

7. Did the theorist confidently claim universality for his theory/theories?

    7.1. Cite the statements made by the theorist and/or by others.

    7.2. Did his claims ever get qualified later?

    7.3. Who were the audiences for whom this was done (identify some meetings of academic associations, etc.)

        7.3.1. Were the reactions positive/ negative/indifferent?

        7.3.2. Were the claims published?

8. Have the theory/theories ever been tested empirically by the theorist or others? If so, what were the results?

    8.1. Explain the tests conducted by the theorist, if any.

        8.1.1. Describe the methods.

        8.1.2. How were the generalizations attained?

        8.1.3. What results were produced?

        8.1.4. How were the findings presented?

8.2. Describe the tests replicated by others, if any.

    8.2.1. Describe the methods.

    8.2.2. What results were produced?

    8.2.3. Give information on research reports: availability, records, raw data, replication of research.

9. Locate any evidence showing the importance and influence of the theorist's major theory/theories.

    9.1. What schools/programs were modeled upon the theorist's theory/theories?

    9.2. What curriculum designs did the theorist inspire?

    9.3. Describe the experiments based on the theory/theories.

    9.4. Did students of the subject subscribe to this theory/theories on the basis of opinion or evidence?

10. Did the theorist or others give suggestions about how the theory/theories might be used?

    10.1. What did the theorist say about how the theory/theories might be applied?

        10.1.1. What kind of guidelines on the application of the theory/theories did the theorist give?

        10.1.2. What parts constitute expected requirements?

10.2.   What precautions did the theorist consider necessary in applying the theory/theories?

10.3.   What precautions have others suggested?

10.4.   What did the theorist think could be expected from application of the theory/theories?

10.5.   What current projects are based partly or completely on the theory/theories?

INDEX

103